the
flying
camel

the flying camel

Essays on Identity by Women of North African and Middle Eastern Jewish Heritage

Edited by
Loolwa Khazzoom

SEAL PRESS

THE FLYING CAMEL: *Essays on Identity by Women of North African and Middle Eastern Jewish Heritage*

© 2003 by Loolwa Khazzoom

Published by
Seal Press
An Imprint of Avalon Publishing Group Incorporated
245 West 17th St., 11th Floor
New York, NY 10011

A different version of "The Life and Times of Ruth of the Jungle" by Ruth Knafo Setton first appeared in *The Jewish Quarterly*, under the name "Homing Pigeon." Permission by *The Jewish Quarterly* and author.

A different version of "Feathers and Hair" by Farideh Dayanim Goldin first appeared in *Wedding Song: Memoirs of an Iranian Jewish Woman* (Brandeis University Press, 2003) by Farideh Goldin. Permission by author.

"Breaking the Silence" by Ella Shohat, Mira Eliezer, Tikva Levy first appeared in Hebrew in *HILA News* Vol. 50 and in English in *News From Within* 10:8, August 1994, under the name "Breaking the Silence: My Oppression as a Mizrahi Woman." Permission by HILA, *News From Within* and authors.

A different version of "Reflections of an Arab Jew" by Ella Shohat first appeared in *Movement Research: Performance Journal* #5 (Fall/Winter, 1992) p.8, under the name "Dislocated Identities: Reflections of an Arab Jew." Permission by author.

A different version of "Illusion in Assimilation" Henriette Dahan Kalev first appeared in *Israel Studies Journal* Vol. 6 p. 1-14, under the name "You're So Pretty, You Don't Look Moroccan." Permission by Indiana University Press.

Library of Congress Cataloging-in-Publication Data is available.

ISBN 1-58005-095-6

9 8 7 6 5 4 3 2 1

Designed by Paul Paddock
Printed in Canada
Distributed by Publishers Group West

Dedication

To the spirits of the female ancestors whose presence I felt singing with me as I led prayers for the first-ever egalitarian Mizrahi/Sephardi High Holy Day services in 1997: to those of you who tried to lead but were not allowed, to those of you who did not feel the courage or self-worth to try, and to those of you whose spirits were broken so early on you did not even have the desire.

To the spirit of Ofra Haza, who was my first role model and an inspiration to Mizrahi and Sephardi women and girls around the world.

To all the Mizrahi and Sephardi girls and women who were and who are silenced: May those of you who have passed on find voice through our words. May those of you who are alive find inspiration and courage through them.

To My Fighting Child Spirit, who refuses to give up or give in, and to my Creator for gifting me with an abundance of courage, vision, and will: Thank You.

You must do the thing
you think you cannot do.

—Eleanor Roosevelt

Contents

INTRODUCTION

Among the piles of boxes in the attic, I found a long, black, silk robe with the initials "LK" embroidered in red on the back. I examined the garment, holding it close to my body. It had to be mine, given the initials. But I had no memory of it. I could not have worn it as a child; even at my height of five feet, seven inches, it was too long for me.

LK. Suddenly it dawned on me: My grandmother, LouLou Khazzoom, must have thought it charmingly exotic to embroider her initials in English, instead of in Judeo-Arabic, her mother tongue. This was her *abayah*, the full-body covering Muslim women wear in general and Jewish women wore when going outdoors in Iraq. I slipped my arms through the sleeves and lifted over my head what I had mistaken as the neckline in back.

When I looked in the mirror, two brown eyes peered back at me through a mass of black material around my face. As I felt the weight of the full-body veil, I also felt resentment rising inside. I imagined walking through the streets of Baghdad, yearning deeply to throw my head back and laugh, sing, twirl around in the sunshine. I wondered if my grandmother experienced this resentment, retreating to a shrouded inner world day after day when she stepped outside.

Who was my grandmother? All the stories I had heard about her were through my father. Like the story about how my grandfather, madly in love with her, took her across the Tigris River during a flood in the city. Alone in a boat for hours, they were required to get engaged when they returned to shore—my grandfather's plan all along. *How did my* grandmother *feel about it,* I began to wonder as I grew up. Did she even feel entitled to have an opinion on the matter? I will never know; she died before I was born.

As I entered my adult years, I realized that my relationship to my entire family was filtered through my father's lens—often second hand, through *his* father's lens. "Family" as I knew it was essentially a matriarchy, with six aunts and one surviving uncle, yet I knew nothing about the female version of family life. My mother knew nothing about women's experience of Jewish life in Iraq, as she grew up Christian in Illinois.

Once I managed to clear out the father-filter in my head, I found most of my aunts speaking through a father-filter of their own, accepting and embracing "the woman's role" with impunity and condemning me for not following it. The traditional veil, it seemed, not only covered the bodies of the Khazzoom women; it also permeated our souls.

I have found this veil appearing in many forms, touching each layer of the experience of North African and Middle Eastern Jewish women. It has appeared externally and internally, physically and metaphorically. For Jewish women, donning the veil reflected not only men's codes in relation to women but also Muslim codes in relation to Jews. Since the Muslim conquest of the region about 1,300 years ago, Jews indigenous to North Africa and the Middle

East suddenly found themselves second-class citizens, beholden to the laws of Islam—including the injunction that women wear veils. In this context, the veil also acted as a symbol of the struggle to pass as someone else or stand tall as oneself, at times a life-and-death choice for Jews in the region.

Today, North African and Middle Eastern Jewish women continue to live in the shadows of metaphoric veils—sheets of material others throw over us in attempts to shroud our identity and history. In a world where Jewish is synonymous with Central and Eastern European, where North African/Middle Eastern is synonymous with Arab Muslim, where "of color" is synonymous with "not Jewish," and where communities are generally represented through their men, our mere existence threatens to destroy the foundation of numerous identity constructs as society knows them today. People try desperately to reconfigure *us,* lest they should have to reconfigure fashionable uniting and dividing lines.

As a result, the world has heard little or nothing about Jewish women from North Africa and the Middle East. For starters, few people know our names—*Mizrahiot* and *Sepharadiot.* A veil of invisibility obscures our history (herstory) as well.

Mizrahiot are those whose foremothers lived in North Africa and the Middle East since Sarah, the Jewish matriarch, emerged from Mesopotamia (pre-Babylonian Empire) 4,000 years ago, crossing the Euphrates River into the Promised Land to the west. Her Jewish descendants lived on this land, first as the tribal nation of Israel and then as the ancient kingdom of Israel, over a period of about 1,500 years.

In 722 BCE, the Assyrians conquered Northern Israel, using tactics that forced the Israelites to flee and scatter throughout the region. In 586 BCE, the Babylonian Empire (ancient Iraq) conquered Yehuda (Judah), the southern region of ancient Israel. Babylonians occupied the land and exiled the *Yehudim* (Jews), as captives into Babylon. Some fifty years later, the Persian Empire (ancient Iran) conquered the Babylonian Empire and allowed the Jews to return home to the land of Israel. Though offered freedom under Persian rule, most Jews were daunted by the task of rebuilding a society that lay in ruins, and remained in Babylon. Over the next millennia, they either stayed where they were or migrated to neighboring lands in the region (including the land of Israel, which centuries later the Romans renamed Palestina), or countries in Central and East Asia.

Sepharadiot are women descending from the line of Jews who chose to return and rebuild their homeland after the Persian Empire conquered the Babylonian Empire. About half a millennium later, the Roman Empire conquered ancient Israel for the second time, massacring most of the nation and taking the bulk of the remainder as slaves to Rome. Once the Roman Empire crumbled, descendants of these captives migrated throughout the European continent. Many settled in Spain (Sepharad) and Portugal, where they thrived until the Spanish Inquisition and expulsion of 1492 and the Portuguese Inquisition and expulsion shortly thereafter.

During these periods, the Christian governments either burned Jews alive, forcibly converted them to Christianity, or forced them out of the country. Jews who fled settled predominantly throughout the Mediterranean regions of the Ottoman (Turkish) Empire, as well as Central and South America. The *Sepharadiot* who fled to North African and Middle Eastern lands merged with the *Mizrahiot*, Jewish women whose families had been living there for thousands of years.

In the early twentieth century, severe violence against Jews forced communities throughout the region to flee once again, arriving as refugees predominantly in Israel, France, the United Kingdom, and the Americas. In Israel, North African and Middle Eastern Jews were the majority of the Jewish population for decades, with numbers as high as 70 percent, until the mass Russian immigration of the 1990s. We are now half of the Jewish population. Throughout the rest of the world, we have a strong presence in metropolitan areas—Paris, Brooklyn, Montreal, London, Mexico City, and Los Angeles.

From these diverse communities across the globe, seventeen courageous *Mizrahiot* and *Sepharadiot* have stepped forth from the shadows, daring to speak out. They possess the refreshing viewpoint of those on the edge, insiders and outsiders to many different worlds. They refuse to be defined as "other" or "less than" by any of the communities to which they belong. Their vivid, gripping narratives sweep readers into a journey of discovery, unveiling the rich, multicolored texture of identities commonly portrayed as one-dimensional or black and white.

The contributors come from numerous professions, diverse class backgrounds, and various sexual orientations. They are single women, partnered women, mothers, and grandmothers, from religious and secular homes. Pushed and pulled by the strong currents of today's identity politics, they remain steadfast, charting a clear course for themselves and setting the rules of their own games: Bahareh Mobasseri Rinsler launches a sexual revolt among Iranian Jewish women; Gina Bublil Waldman single-handedly rescues her family from assassination in Libya; Mira Eliezer, Tikva Levy, and Ella Shohat storm the ranks of Israel's feminist movement; Yael Arami forges a path for religious *Mizrahiot;* and Rachel Wahba sounds the cry of North African and Middle Eastern Jewish refugees worldwide.

As Lital Levy notes in her essay, "How the Camel Found Its Wings," women of North African and Middle Eastern Jewish heritage "are not what our parents were and definitely not what our grandparents were . . . Like it or not, we are hybrids of past and present, old and new, East and West."

Drawing on the imagery of a flying camel whose wings are broken, Lital shares the process of picking up shattered pieces of her Iraqi Jewish heritage and blending them with other parts of her being—thus re-membering her camel's wings and giving flight to a new, integrated identity. "Our identities," Lital notes, "perhaps the only thing truly our own, can be fashioned as we ourselves choose, paving a unique path to our future—a path that is part inheritance and part creativity, baseline, and improvisation."

For all the women in this collection, our identities have been shattered and need to be rebuilt. The beauty and appropriateness of Lital's metaphor are among the many reasons why I named this anthology *The Flying Camel*.

When I first came up with the idea of compiling an anthology of North African and Middle Eastern Jewish feminists, the only women I knew who fit the bill were my sister and myself. Although others like us existed, there was no cohesive community and not much of a network. As a result, collecting stories for this book was a mighty task.

Part of the struggle was an integral piece of our story: Only recently, our families were scattered to the four corners of the earth, and we had not quite recuperated from the traumatic upheaval. During the ten years I worked on this book, however, I saw magical transformations taking place. Not only did the process of searching for and gathering stories acquaint me with phenomenal *Mizrahiot* and *Sepharadiot* worldwide, but I was able to participate in their own efforts to organize and mobilize us. I attended the first international conference for African and Middle Eastern Jewish women; I displayed my work in the first Israeli art exhibit of *Mizrahiot* and *Sepharadiot;* I co-organized and co-led the first egalitarian services in our community worldwide, for Rosh Hashanah and Yom Kippur; and I presented at the first Israeli feminist conference where *Mizrahiot* and *Sepharadiot* had won the fight for equal representation.

I have been exhilarated and honored to stand with other *Mizrahiot* and *Sepharadiot* on the forefronts of change. Of course, even with all our progress, we still have much farther to go. Jewish women's literature has begun to show a smattering of consciousness about our diversity, but I want to see it move beyond tokenism. I want to see Arab women's literature include us, period. I want to see the multicultural movement in America reflect the faces and voices of Jews of color. I want to see college courses on North Africa and the Middle East include our stories, and I want to see seminary courses on Jewish religion include our texts. I want to stop hearing my community being referred to as barbaric, primitive, uneducated, dirty, and violent or as different, unusual, mysterious, fascinating, and exotic.

I pray that this book will be one more step toward lifting the veil off our collective bodies, psyches, and souls. I pray that we finally will be recognized, accepted, and loved for who we are. I pray that we finally will throw our heads back and laugh, sing, twirl around in the sunshine. Just as LouLou Khazzoom may have wanted to do, one hundred years ago.

Insh'allah.

Loolwa Khazzoom
Be'er Sheva
July 2003

RUTH KNAFO SETTON

THE LIFE AND TIMES OF RUTH OF THE JUNGLE

m y first memory is of looking into my grandfather's smiling face as he winds a rose around my ear. We were on his roof terrace, a paradise he constructed for himself in Safi. In Morocco, the roof is traditionally the woman's sphere and the street the man's, but my grandfather turned the world upside down. He built a low wall around his roof, so the women on the adjoining roofs could not watch him. In the early days, he glared at them with fierce eyebrows and flaring nostrils, until they backed away.

The moment he returned home from work—which he detested, no matter the job—he would tear off his street clothes and put on a snow-white *djellabah* that fell to his ankles. Then he would climb the narrow, winding staircase to the roof. It was his refuge from the world below—the world where a Jew survived by being invisible, walking with eyes lowered, hiding every truth within. It was where my grandfather could study, play the lute, compose music, and write poetry in classical Arabic. Where he could brave the notorious Safi wind that carved a cavity in his soul, a hollow yearning for freedom.

Where he could raise his pigeons—fifty, in two huge brass cages, the gates never locked, or even closed. When my mother asked why, he replied, "You don't hold someone by locking them behind bars."

My mother struggled to understand that notion, as she passed through the gate that marked off the Jewish Quarter from the rest of the town. The gate no longer was locked, but the sultan still held the key: It could be locked at any time. *Are we the sultan's birds?* my mother wondered. Every time she left the Jewish Quarter, on her way to and from my brothers' Alliance Israelite school, she was on the lookout for the Arab boys who threw stones at the Jewish kids. But my mother was not allowed on Sa'adia's roof terrace. Neither was my grandmother. Only I, his first grandchild.

Sa'adia Cohen, of the flaming red hair and brilliant green-gold eyes—tall, handsome and lusty, a pirate blown into our claustrophobic, tiny streets, who brought memories of the sea with him. He played the lute on his roof. He sang in Arabic, Judeo-Arabic, and Hebrew at weddings and parties. He smoked *kief* while with his friends, and cigarettes while brooding over his poems.

When he set the pigeons free that last time, he didn't have to tell them; they sensed it. He tied secret kabbalistic messages to their legs. He stood there on the roof, surrounded by his roses and geraniums, his books and lute, a silver teapot, and the small Berber carpet on which he sat and meditated. The sea wind blew as he urged the pigeons to go, to fly away, find a new home, explore the world.

I close my eyes now and see Sa'adia standing there, a mountain of a man, a dreamer who created his own small universe. Some of the pigeons were reluctant to leave him, this man who seemed to understand the soul of birds, who flew with them—even though he remained on the roof while they soared. Sa'adia admired those who left quickly, with no sentimentality—no circling and hovering in useless longing to return. And so he hardened his heart, stood against the wind, and watched his birds fill the sky with a hiss and whir as they disappeared, until the two large brass cages were empty. The cages remained on the roof, gates swinging open and shut in the wind, until Sa'adia carried them down the narrow circular staircase that he built himself, with his own hands. I built the stairway to my soul, he was fond of saying.

Later, long after I had left with my parents to America, Sa'adia replaced the pigeons—those birds who knew him, who returned to him after their every flight—with a large aquarium filled with strange species of fish. "I have to watch life," he wrote to my mother. When I returned to Morocco for the first time, I accompanied my mother; she was scared to go back alone. There I saw the grandfather I remembered only in dream and memory: He lay in bed, nose large as a bird beak, hair sparse and white. As I approached him, he held out a blue-veined hand from which flesh hung. He breathed in rasps and ragged coughs. When our hands touched, he smiled. I cried in my heart, tears knocking against walls I didn't know existed, breaking through doors.

My mother motioned for me to turn around. On the wall facing my grandfather was a painting of me as a child. My uncle, my mother's younger brother, had painted me from a photograph. My grandfather's last words were spoken to me. *"Mon tresor,"* he said. My treasure. In the small house, *shiva*—the seven days of mourning—began. The women in black, the men unshaven and barefoot. The professional mourners—black

3

ravens—terrified me with their unearthly wails, their faces seared with their fingernails as they slashed at themselves and pulled their hair, shrieking with raw, uncontrolled grief.

I wandered through the house. In each room, people sat on the floor and recalled Sa'adia in Arabic and French. The legends about him. The women he conquered with a glance. The music with which he charmed enemies. The words he wove into nets and wings that swooped and soared. Women bemoaned his constant smoking, the cigarettes that led to his lung cancer. The nights he stayed awake alone on the roof doing who knows what. His other women. The mystery and emotional solitude of the man. In every room, my grandfather remained unknown. An enigma.

Freedom, my father had said. *We're going to America to be free.* We followed his sister, who had married an American G.I.—his sister, a woman slowly punished and exiled by her husband's Christian family, until she no longer remembered who she was. They mocked her Jewish faith. They locked her outside in the snow on Christmas. "A Jew shouldn't participate in our festivities," they said. Her husband insulted her constantly and beat her, even when she was pregnant.

By the time my sister and I came to know her, my aunt was a witch out of horror stories. She would wait for us after school, and as we began to walk home, surrounded by kids from our classes, she would emerge from behind the trees, red hair wild and tangled, screaming, "They're Jews! They're from Morocco! They're lying to everyone! Jews! Morocco!"

My sister and I had nightmares about my aunt. We loathed her for years, not understanding until much later that when she exposed us to the hatred of our classmates, she exposed her own pain at being punished for who she was. If we had been telling the truth about being Jews from Morocco, maybe my aunt's attacks would not have carried so much weight. But we had transformed ourselves.

Sick to death of the years of fear and humiliation as a Jew in Morocco, and traumatized by his sister's hellish life with a non-Jew who continued to torture her, my father decided to change his family with a stroke of the wand—from Moroccan Jews to French Christians. France would explain the accent, and the Christian exterior would eliminate centuries of hardship. "Wherever we go as Jews, we're going to suffer," he told me. "Let's start over." Besides, he added, the myth would make it easier for our small-town Pennsylvania-Dutch neighbors to understand us.

But this family turn against Judaism was not simply the result of the anti-Semitism we already had encountered in Morocco and in the States, but because of a more painful, insidious, poisonous hatred and scorn that came from other Jews. When we first arrived in America, my father went to the local synagogue and met with the board of directors. After expressing shock that Jews lived in remote Morocco, they kindly advised him to return to Africa, saying, "There's nothing for your kind here." My father came back home furious, only to find me crying. That day, my teacher had asked me loudly, in front of the class, "Is it true you eat people in Morocco?"

The kids at school then began calling my sister and me "Jungle Jews," and I became afraid to leave the house. My family moved to the adjoining town, wrenching ourselves from our dark, bloody, religious heritage and disassociating ourselves from the somber mosque'd landscape from which we had emerged. Too much to cram down unwary throats: Moroccan and Jewish. So we made it "pretty" and "civilized," until our story hardened and fastened about us with the implacability of myth.

In an inspired touch, Safi became Paris. In a reductio ad absurdum, Jewish became Christian and then dwindled to nothing. The disguise: from horned usurers storming out of a savage jungle into placid, sandy-haired farmers. An attempt as ridiculous as it was doomed, as impossible as my childhood desire to become a seagull.

I examine frequently the confusion of identity this switch caused, the daily terror at being found out. I lived in my own perpetual fear of an Inquisition. Torquemada, the dreaded torturer of the Spanish Inquisition, indeed stalked me in the form of John, a neighborhood boy. Cold-eyed and chinless, he suspected my family from the start and cross-examined me, trying to trap me in my lie.

"What church do you go to?" John asked one day.

"Uh, the one on the corner," I stammered.

"What corner?"

"The one with the big cross. You know."

"That's my church. How come I never saw you there?"

"We're very busy. We only go sometimes."

"You're going to go to hell! My dad says you're kikes. That's why you don't go to church. You better come to Sunday school with me and my sister next Sunday. Unless you're scared," he added.

"Scared?" I replied. "Me? Ha!"

I went to church with him. I felt eyes on me from all sides, from the congregants to the Gothic arches to the pale-eyed Jesus and Madonna. Everyone watched and saw through me. I was the sinful one, the dark, evil one, the Jew from hateful Morocco—wherever that was. In my soul I knew I was no

Christian from Paris. No matter how carefully I disguised myself, my *pieds noirs* peeked through. And yet, I carried on with the disguise, pretending until I was in high school that I was a Christian—an honorable and true American. I belonged in America: I dated non-Jews, had no knowledge of "Jewish" food (gefilte fish), rarely entered a synagogue, and never went to a bat mitzvah.

Then the Six-Day War erupted in our living room. I remember kneeling in front of the TV, stunned by the faces of the soldiers, by the vision of Moshe Dayan with his eyepatch, by the shy pride and glowing eyes of the young men. *I am a Jew,* I realized, just like that. *I can't lie anymore. I can't keep running.*

I broke off my engagement to the son of a minister and flew to Israel. From the moment I landed at Lod Airport and breathed in the heat, dust, flowers, human sweat, and desire, I knew that Israel wasn't just a country; she was mine, the way no other country ever could be. She was Jewish, Mediterranean, smeling of sand, sea, and roses: my memory come to life.

In Israel, I was home and proud to be a Jew. But I soon learned that Israel was an Ashkenazi nation constructed in the Middle East. We Mizrahim were, in Ben-Gurion's words, their "coolie labor"—monkeys from Africa; uneducated, primitive beasts with no need for education or plumbing. I found myself passing yet again, this time as an American Jew (hence, Ashkenazi), but I could not bear the lie.

On a date, when the young Israeli man began mocking the accent Mizrahim have when they speak Hebrew, I said coldly, "I am Moroccan." He thought I was joking. When I applied for a job as an English teacher—by far the most qualified person, holding a master's degree in English—I did not get the job, but a high-school graduate from California did. Why? Mr. Goldberg, the director of the language institute, told me bluntly, "I don't hire Moroccans. Some of my best friends are Moroccans, but you're not good workers. You're not reliable."

I returned to the States, determined to find out more about what it meant to be a Jew from Morocco. Suleika was my way in. Her name caught me, illuminated like the letters in a medieval manuscript. I tracked down her story: A seventeen-year-old Moroccan Jewish girl of almost unearthly beauty, Suleika was beheaded by the sultan of Morocco in Fez in 1834 for refusing to convert to Islam. Although all the variations of the story of her brief, tragic life end with her execution, the road there differs with whoever is telling the tale.

I spent the next fifteen years researching her life, working on a novel about her, *The Road to Fez,* at the same time coming to terms with my own identity. Through those years I confronted American Jewish self-hatred, often directed against Mizrahim/Sephardim. Often, I was told that our experiences did not matter; that our history was painless, our Hebrew accents ugly, our customs barbaric. An American publisher returned an early draft of *The Road to Fez* with a note, "You write well. Next time try writing about the real Jews."

The real Jews. Who were they? Who are they? My ancestor, Maklouf Knafo, one of the legendary *nisrafim* (Burnt Ones), a man who chose to burn to death on a sunny spring morning in 1790 in Oufran, rather than convert to Islam? My uncle, who was tortured in a Moroccan jail for suspicious (i.e., Zionist) activities? Another uncle, a parachutist in the Israeli army, a P.O.W., tortured by the Egyptians, sent back with the mental abilities of a child and constant headaches and nightmares?

Was a real Jew my mother, who cooked couscous and listened to Jo Amar and tried to keep Moroccan Jewish traditions alive, while my father ran as fast as he could from everything he had been? My aunt, who grew up a Jew in Morocco, literally and symbolically known as "the lowest of the low," and came to America for freedom, only to find she was still considered "the lowest of the low"—prompting her to attack two little girls, maybe the only creatures even lower than she? Suleika, a seventeen-year-old girl with her entire life in front of her, offered the world if she would convert to Islam but beheaded on another sunny day in Morocco, because she couldn't change who she was?

For Suleika, to convert and live a lie would be a death-in-life—the same death-in-life I had been living. I realized that my childhood and adolescence were nothing more than the Converso lifestyle, transferred to a small Pennsylvania town. I had been a little girl told to say the words, "I am a Christian." As if words are enough to change who you are. Odd as it may seem, I was brought up in the most Jewish way imaginable—denying my Jewishness in order to survive.

I watched them lower my grandfather into the ground in the Jewish cemetery. The wind blew sharply. Pigeons circled my head. My tears were frozen inside. A cousin with a blue bandanna tied around his forehead screamed like a wounded beast. The graves were piled helter-skelter, in no apparent order, up a steep grassy hill. The wind blew us back as we climbed it.

My great-grandmother, a wrinkled mask from which two eyes of astounding beauty peered out, wailed the entire way up the hill, "What has become of my beauty?" she said of my grandfather. "Oh, my lost beauty! My beauty, where are you?

Why did you leave me?" The men wore sneakers, their unshaven faces adding a sinister, romantic aura to the wild cemetery and the fierce wind. As they threw dirt over my grandfather, I remembered my mother telling me how he had longed to go to Israel, to dig his fingers into the dirt—"the same dirt David touched." To press his ear against the stone of the wall of Solomon's Temple and hear the words of captured dreams. To wade into the Mediterranean, naked and free, "until I touch the black line," he had said. "To go deeper and farther until there is nowhere to advance but directly into the past."

I close my eyes and see my grandfather finish twining the rose around my ear then kiss my forehead. Leaving his kingdom above the world, I descend his winding staircase on my chubby little legs. By the time I reach the bottom step, I am ready to open the front door and step out onto the street—a woman bare-faced, open-hearted, secrets sifting through my fingers.

FARIDEH DAYANIM GOLDIN

fEATHERS AND HAIR

Plucking chickens the kosher way is quite an art. According to the laws of *kashrut,* a chicken should not be cooked or even brought close to a source of heat until it is *kashered*—bled, salted, and rinsed. The use of fire to sear feathers or hot water to loosen quills is absolutely forbidden. Poultry processors today use the force of air to pluck feathers for kosher markets; but when I lived in Iran, during the '60s and '70s, this job had to be done manually.

Chickens were brought to the women of a household right after the chickens were slaughtered, which usually happened in the backyard. For each chicken, the *shohed* recited the requisite *bracha,* plucked a patch of feathers from underneath the chicken's neck, pulled back its head, and slit its throat. He then threw the chicken on the grass to do its dance of death, banging itself against the thorny rose bushes. The chickens were still warm when we started to pluck them.

The largest surface of a chicken carcass has fine feathers that are easy to pull. On rare occasions, when there were more than the one or two chickens customary for *Shabbat* or holidays, I could get a rhythm going and clean the chickens quite fast. The larger feathers, however, are embedded deep in the flesh and were difficult to pluck—particularly the wings, where the skin was delicate and tore easily. The fatty backside of a chicken was even worse: The long quills pulled out fat and blood, making everything greasy and sticky. Fine feathers clung to my hands, arms, legs, and clothes wherever the fat splattered. Worse yet, the quills often broke. To pull them out, I had to trap the embedded pieces between the edge of a small knife and my thumb, being careful not to cut my finger. My mother, like other adult women, seldom worried about cutting herself. Her hands were already rough from housework, so the knife made small dents on her thick calluses, but rarely drew blood.

Weddings, especially, tested our chicken-cleaning skills. Since we had no refrigeration back then, "pluckers" had to clean and cook a large pile of chickens quickly, leaving little time to clean up and get dressed for the wedding party. I must have set a record cleaning chickens for my cousin Ziba's wedding. Hired cooks boiled water in industrial-sized pots on top of wood-burning mud stoves, impatiently waiting for the chickens. Burlap bags of Basmati rice (which, weeks earlier, we had cleaned of pebbles, incidental grains of legumes, mung beans, wheat, and sometimes a dead beetle or two) were already triple-washed and ready to be boiled in salted water, steamed, and mixed with fava beans, herbs, barberries, pistachios, saffron, and carrots.

A few men from the bride's and groom's families gathered with the rabbi in a secluded room on the second floor to negotiate and argue the terms of my cousin's wedding contract: the amount of the *mehrieh* and the dowry. Once in a while, the dispute became heated, and a man from this or that side of the family left the negotiating table in protest, announcing that the wedding was off.

Women stopped their work until another man came to appease the disgruntled one, convincing him to rejoin the negotiations. Then the women went on with their own preparations, dividing into two groups. The first, the more prestigious family members and guests—my grandmother, the mothers of the bride and groom, some aunts, and many known women of the community—were led to a room decorated for a pre-wedding party, replete with large pillows on the Persian carpets, to lean against while sitting cross-legged on the floor. Some of my female cousins were given trays of sweets, limeade, and *sharbat* to pass around. Bags of *noghl* were placed around the room for the women to munch on and to shower the bride with, as they covered their mouths with their *chadors* and ululated, *Kililili!*

The second group of women—including my mother, my sister, myself, the washer-woman, and her daughter—sat outside on low stools in the brick-paved backyard, cleaning mounds of chickens. I sat by the dead chickens, angry, resentful, and hurt for being excluded from the party room, missing whatever was going on in there. But I kept my feelings to myself. Good girls did not complain.

My mother was born in Hamedan, far from my father's hometown of Shiraz. Being a woman, and born at a time of oppression and extreme poverty for most Iranian Jews, my mother had been of no use to her parents, just another mouth to feed. In addition to worrying about the harshness of their own lives, my grandparents worried that my mother could get raped or kidnapped by anti-Semitic hoodlums in her city of birth. Before reaching puberty, when my mother was barely thirteen years old, my grandparents gave their only daughter away to my father, whom they had met for the first time just a few weeks earlier, when he had knocked at their door to ask for my mother's hand in marriage. He took her away to live with his family, at a time when traveling was time-consuming, expensive, and arduous. Throughout her marriage, having no family for protection, my mother remained an outsider in my father's family—a lonely and silent woman.

My mother's problems were not just her own. As I grew older, being her first child and being female, my fate became increasingly connected to hers. Repeatedly, just like my mother, I felt as if I were a stranger among my own family, as if I were still covered by the amniotic fluid that had protected me in my mother's womb—a fluid that no longer offered me warmth and safety. Instead, its old stench kept me at a distance from my cousins, who should have been my equals, my pals.

Noticing the look of disappointment on my face as she gave me the job, my grandmother said that it was a *mitzvah* to pluck chickens for a wedding, and that it would bring me good luck, a good husband. But her words did not keep me from hating the hard, dirty work. I knew that by the time the chickens were feathered, gutted, and cleaned, I would be covered in chicken feathers, fat, blood, and excrement, and I would smell like them, too.

I had finished plucking my third bird and was reaching toward the mound of white, orange, and black feathers for my fourth, when I noticed the *band andaz* entering the hallway, a small basket of thread in one hand and a colorful *chador* around her face, held by the other hand. She entered the room with much pomp and circumstance, let go of her body covering in the presence of the women, cupped her mouth and ululated, *Kililili!* Her arrival sent a wave of loud ululation from the party room towards us. We imitated the women's cries of joy like an echo, as we plucked away.

I had seen this woman before. I had watched her hold one end of a piece of string between her teeth and loop the other end, putting it next to a woman's face, legs, or arms and pulling it, swiftly removing hair. Body hair was an obsession not only with the Jews, but with most Iranians. Middle Eastern women tend to have dark and sometimes abundant body hair, the growth and darkening of which is often synonymous with the loss of childhood beauty and innocence. Its removal makes women more appealing to Iranian men—especially in that generation, whose men preferred younger women. My cousin Ziba had some facial hair close to her hairline. I knew the *band andaz* was going to make her face smooth and her legs soft.

I kept plucking away at the chickens, all the while listening to the noises from the party room. The ululation continued, and occasionally I heard a subdued moan from my cousin, when a particularly stubborn hair was pulled. We were almost to the end of the pile of chickens when we heard heart-wrenching screams from Ziba. Even the loud ululation could not muffle them. I was horrified and poised to jump off my stool to run and help my cousin, but my mother pulled me down with a knowing smile on her face. What was happening? I dared not ask. My mother and the rest of the women in my group joined in drowning out Ziba's cries by adding their own sounds of ululation.

I had been taught that *najeeb* girls, decent and modest young women, could not ask questions; we had to be *sharm-roo,* quiet and bashful. I had learned to watch and listen quietly, in the hope that information would come along voluntarily. This time, I did not have to wait long. My mother left briefly to fetch water to spray the feathers, to keep them from flying. One of the cleaning women, who obviously was from the "lower class" and did not have our upper-class inhibitions, bent toward me. Using a derogatory word, she whispered, "They are doing her private parts!" She then giggled hysterically, covering her mouth with her feather-laden hand.

There I was plucking chickens, while the hierarchy of the community was plucking my cousin's pubic hair! I could not get the humiliating image out of my mind: Ziba with her legs spread in front of all those women modestly covered in *chadors,* while someone plucked hair from a part of her body that was so private we were not even allowed to name it. Angry, afraid, and worried about Ziba, I plucked recklessly, ruining the skin of the next few chickens.

I had seen the *band andaz* at work on women's faces, legs, and arms. I had seen naked bodies of married women with shaven private parts at the *hamam,* the public baths. Neither vision had disturbed me. What frightened me was the public spectacle of this pre-wedding ceremony, which to me signified a woman's loss of self-determination and control over her own destiny. This initiation into the culture of female conformity horrified me, although it delighted the other women. I was only fourteen, a year older than my mother at her wedding, and three years younger than Ziba. Instead of accepting the custom as a wonderful show of support and camaraderie, as other women were doing, I felt lost. I worried that my life would spin out of my control as I grew older.

A few weeks later, I asked Ziba about the event. "It hurt like nothing I have ever experienced," she replied. "Even the *band andaz* said she had never seen anyone bleed so badly!" Ziba spoke with a pride I could not understand. For years, the experience stayed on the surface of my consciousness, rarely leaving me during my daily activities. Why, I would wonder, did Ziba's mother and grandmother allow the ceremony? Did they not have the same experience? How could they watch her in so much pain? How could they allow the humiliation?

The answer sank in slowly and bitterly, throughout the years I lived in Iran: My mother was dragging me down with her, into a dark abyss. All mothers, in fact, were dragging down their daughters. I felt appalled and horrified thinking of Ziba's mother and grandmother (who was also my grandmother) passing on the customs of torture and degradation to the next generation. *To please whom?* I wondered. I felt hopeless and helpless. I was afraid to discuss my thoughts with anyone—my mother, grandmother, or friends. I felt that the plucking was just a symbol of our mothers subjugating us, the daughters; forcing us to walk in our mothers' paths, so as to justify what was done to them by their own mothers.

Years later, however, I came to feel that maybe the only power our mothers had was the power to implement the rules of patriarchy. Sympathy replaced my anger, and I even felt respect for our mothers' zeal to survive.

At the end of the *band andazi* party, my grandmother stopped by to see how the chicken-cleaning had gone. She blessed me, *"Insh'allah nesbatesh be shomas, khoshbakhti, khoobi, khoshi!"* (I pray for the same happiness and good life for you.) And I, who had learned to stay silent, lost control of my tongue. *"Khoda nakoneh!"* I spat. (May it not be God's will!) In the silence that followed, looks of horror spread over every face, including that of my father, who had just walked over to check on us.

A daughter's wedding day is the ultimate desire for Iranian Jewish parents. I knew I did not want it, not this way. But which way? I did not know. I recognized myself as an oddity, an irregular, a loner, a defiant girl. My heart went out to my parents, knowing that I was an embarrassment and an outsider. I felt frightened, not knowing what was going to become of me. What, after all, can become of one who does not belong, who loathes and rejects the customs?

At my cousin's wedding, I did not know if I could ever find the courage and determination to defy the standards of life for a Jewish woman from a small town in Iran. Not being able to fight the traditions, the *band andazi* being just a small example, I left the country in 1975, four years before an Islamic revolution made life for women and Jews even more unbearable than it already had been.

A decade after my cousin's wedding, I married my Ashkenazi husband in the United States I so desperately wanted to distance myself from my past, my culture, and my country of birth that I eliminated even the smallest trace of my own heritage from the ceremony. I walked down the aisle American style. The chickens were not plucked by anyone I knew; they did not even look like birds. Breast of chicken stuffed with wild rice was on the reception menu, not Iranian stew made with chopped herbs; not aromatic rice topped with crusty, saffron-colored *tadig*. The music my fiancé and I selected had an Eastern European flavor. With one exception, none of my Iranian aunts living in the United States attended the wedding to sing *vasoonak* for me, the traditional Shirazi Jewish wedding songs.

My wedding was Ashkenazi American, all the way. If I have any regret about my wedding day, as beautiful as it was, it is the fact that I allowed my fear of and disgust with some customs to erase all the others.

My grandmother came from Iran a few days before the wedding. She brought her *ghalyoun* (waterpipe) and Iranian tobacco. She sat cross-legged on the floor and sipped hot tea flavored with fresh mint, a sugar lump in the back of her cheek. She took a puff on her waterpipe and entertained her hybrid American grandchildren with the gurgle of the water at its base. The men ran inside for their cameras.

While the men were gone, my grandmother put her lips to my aunt's ear, signaled toward me, and in a loud whisper asked, "Has she taken care of the stuff?" Initially, I did not understand what she meant, but when I realized the meaning of her words, a rush of blood shot through my body like a jolt of lightning. The memory of my cousin's wedding flooded my mind with a momentary feeling of despair and disbelief. How could I have forgotten?

I composed myself, and with a smile, replied, "Yes, definitely." And in a small voice she could not hear, I added, "For generations to come."

SOUVENIR FROM LIBYA

I was nineteen years old, working my first summer job at a British engineering company in Tripoli, Libya. One very warm day in the office, as the air conditioner hummed monotonously and I typed some technical documents on my Olivetti typewriter, Mohammed, the company driver, suddenly barged into my office, his eyes full of rage. Banging his fist on my desk, determination in his voice, he barked menacingly, "Don't expect me to take you home today!" Afraid to ask him why, I simply watched the anger seep through his narrowed eyes.

Mohammed turned to leave my office, and one of the company's engineers came in, proclaiming, "Israel is at war with Egypt. It's just come over the radio, haven't you heard? The Israeli army is already in the Sinai desert and is advancing. Pretty soon we shall have to switch to Israeli currency!"

It was June 5, 1967, the beginning of the Six-Day War between Israel and its Arab neighbors. Egypt and four other Arab countries had amassed 100,000 troops, thousands of tanks, and hundreds of jet bombers on Israel's borders. Egypt had closed the international waters of the Straits of Tiran to Israeli ships and kicked out all U.N. peacekeeping forces in the Sinai. Israel was forced to launch a preemptive strike.

For days before the war broke out, we had heard broadcasts from mosques and the Egyptian radio station, inciting fellow Muslims to join the jihad, the so-called holy war, and "drive the Jews into the sea." Just a week earlier, I had been visiting at my aunt Rina's home, when we had heard shouts outside: *"Ya biladi Falistin! Falistin!* (My country, Palestine! Palestine!)"

Thousands of people had taken to the streets, carrying huge anti-Israel banners. My aunt took my cousins and me into her bedroom, closed all the shades, turned off all the lights, and asked us to be very quiet. The crowd marched toward the center of Tripoli for an anti-Israel rally, which ended with the blood-curdling cry, "Death to the Jews!"

Aunt Rina had lived through the 1945 *Mora'ot*—a pogrom in Tripoli where rioting mobs murdered about 150 Jews, attacked and wounded scores more, destroyed five synagogues, and looted nearly all the rest. During the *Mora'ot,* my mother had jumped from her home's rooftop to escape, eventually hiding in the home of a Christian neighbor.

This time, while the demonstrators raged on outside, Aunt Rina sat on the bed and prayed in Hebrew, asking G-d to spare us. When the crowd finally dispersed, I was able to go home.

I was alone in my office, surrounded by strangers—Europeans, mostly British Christians, who could neither comprehend nor understand my fears. Part of me was elated that Israel might win the war, and the other part was apprehensive about the repercussions my family and I would suffer at the hands of the

Libyan government and the masses. Jews in Libya were barely tolerated, living in constant fear of attack even under ordinary circumstances. All this even though Jews had lived in Libya for over 2,500 years, prior to the Arab Muslim conquest that began in the seventh century. In 1492, Spanish and Portuguese Jews fled to Libya, escaping the Spanish Inquisition, and the two separate communities lived together for close to five centuries.

Though Libyan Jews were a vibrant part of society, and despite the fact that we contributed a great deal to the country, Libya persisted in its refusal to grant us citizenship. The Libyan government, moreover, was single-minded in the way it persecuted us: Arbitrary arrests were common, we were stripped of basic human rights, and we were divided from the rest of the Libyan population. I knew a war with Israel would further inflame anti-Jewish sentiment and resentment, giving mobs carte blanche to indulge their worst instincts.

The sharp ring of the telephone broke the heavy silence that had fallen in my office. It was my mother, her voice quivering. "Don't come home! Mobs are rioting in the streets. They have burned your father's warehouse to the ground, and now they have come to burn our house down too. Whatever you do, don't come home, and be careful!" She was crying, panicked.

My eyes clouded with tears, I instinctively ran into my boss's office. "I can't go home, Mr. Hubert. Can you help me?" I pleaded, my voice trembling. A tall, imposing man in his fifties, Mr. Hubert raised his bushy eyebrows and said with impeccable British calm, "Sit down, my dear. Tell me all about it, will you?" I tried to muffle my sobs, putting my hand in front of my mouth. My voice cracked. I paused and calmed my breathing.

"Mr. Hubert, Jewish properties are being plundered and burned everywhere. My mother just called to tell me that a group of demonstrators poured gasoline around the perimeter of our apartment building and prepared to set it ablaze. Our Egyptian neighbor convinced the rioting mob that my family had already left the country and that no Jews were in the building. He said he was the only person living there and cautioned the mob not to burn the home of a Muslim brother."

The demonstrators started to argue with each other, my mother had told me. Since they could not decide whether or not they should burn the building, they agreed to leave a watch guard outside, to make sure my family truly had left.

"My returning home is bound to give my family away," I continued. "I must find a place to hide!" Silence followed, the now-now-dear-let's-see-what-we-can-do kind of silence. I felt churning in the pit of my stomach. Mr. Hubert looked at me with compassion, nodding pensively. I registered with relief that he felt my anguish. He smiled at me encouragingly. "I will see what I can do." I went back to my office to wait. I was swept away by sadness, yearning to be with my family.

Brian, one of the British engineers in the firm, agreed to take me home to stay with him and his wife. As we left, I could see a cloud of smoke coming from the warehouse district where fire was fiercely consuming my father's warehouse, like a wild beast consuming its prey. Thousands of surplus military blankets, tents, boots, and bales of clothing, which my father sold to oil companies throughout Libya, curled up into a dark, black cloud. The building was licked by savage flames that left behind a desolate landscape of charred ruins.

Instead of fighting the flames, firemen stood on top of their engines, raising balled fists and shaking hands with the excited crowd, like members of a soccer team congratulating one another after a good game. The authorities did not pursue the rioters, because they themselves condoned the violence.

Only after several days of rampage and destruction did the authorities finally bring some order and impose a curfew. That is, when the fires spread to Muslim property, the government responded. According to the news that trickled through some foreign broadcasts, reporters who came to Tripoli to cover the riots were sent back, without ever being allowed to leave the airport.

For over three weeks, Brian and his wife Deidre gave me a safe place to live. They took me to work with them and tried their best to make life as normal as possible for me. In the evenings, however, our silence was laced with anxiety. Time stood still.

Each night, I lay in my small bed in their home. Nothing in the room looked familiar, and I felt disoriented. The only things I recognized were my turquoise dress and the sandals I had worn the day I went into hiding.

The prospect of never seeing my family again kept me awake, frightening me more than the drunken violence outside. Shadows gathered in my room in the stillness of the warm night. I dreamt of leaving Libya with my family. My dream filled me with hope, but I never allowed myself to collude with the conspiracy of my dream; I was afraid it might shatter. Predawn light finally caressed me to sleep, and every morning I awoke to the smell of scrambled eggs and buttered white bread.

Brian and Deidre barely knew me and had never met my family, yet they opened their home to me at their own personal risk. People helping or hiding Jews were often threatened and harassed. I felt a heavy responsibility for having placed Brian and Deidre in possible danger.

I often wondered why they helped me. I guess they did it for the same reason my Muslim neighbor saved my family's life:

Despite the evil surrounding us—the murder of innocents, the torching and looting of properties—there was still goodness in some people.

During one of our phone conversations, my mother told me that a school friend of mine had been raped and murdered, and that her family, including eight brothers and sisters, was shot to death. Deborah had been a shy nineteen-year-old, with a mass of brown curls and a slender figure that moved with the elegance of a dancer. As I hid in Brian and Deidre's home, Libyan soldiers had come to Deborah's home, claiming they were going to escort the family to a refugee camp. The soldiers claimed it was for the family's own protection, since it was increasingly dangerous for Jews to stay in their own homes. Deborah's family packed a few belongings, then disappeared forever.

My anxiety grew into profound fear. I shared my feelings with Brian and Deidre, and they began to make plans to secure my family's escape. At a meeting with trusted friends, they discussed plans to smuggle my family and me to safety: A company in England regularly shipped heavy machinery to our engineering company, using very large wooden crates. My family and I would hide in these crates, with a built-in air passage, and clandestinely be shipped out of the country.

Yet during my sleepless nights, I saw my mother suffocating within the walls of a wooden crate. My fear turned into panic. I became consumed with nightmares about being found by the authorities, thrown in jail, and raped by my jailers, or dying a stifling death inside a box. Was this the beginning of the end for us?

As my depression increased, I resolved that I would not be catapulted into a state of utter despair. Instead, I would cope with the tumultuous events around me by developing a strategy to leave the country through legal means.

Like most Jews, my parents were not allowed to have a phone, so they had to go upstairs to our Egyptian neighbor to call me. Brian and Deidre did not have a phone either, which made communication with my parents difficult and infrequent. Sometimes Brian would walk me to his English neighbor's house so I could call my parents—very risky after curfew.

Every day, very early in the morning, Brian and Deidre took me to the office with them, so as not to leave me alone in the house. I had to bend down in the back seat of the car, to avoid being seen by his neighbors and the young Arab kids roaming the streets. Still, one day, as we drove past a group of young boys, they started throwing stones at Brian's car. Luckily, we got away safely.

Toward the end of June, three weeks after I had gone into hiding, I received a call at the office from my cousin Moris. His voice full of excitement, he informed me that the Libyan government was allowing all the Jews to leave the country. The government was freezing all of our assets—properties, lands, homes, and bank accounts—and they would permit us only to take a few suitcases and a little bit of money, but we would be free to go.

At first, I was elated by the prospect of leaving. Soon, however, my happiness clouded over with apprehension of economic uncertainty, and I became angry. Yes, we would be free, but we would have no resources. We would have to emigrate to some country where we would not know anyone, not own anything, and not have any money. We would end up in some country where my family had never been and where the language would be foreign to us. I did not even know where we would end up—England? France? Italy?

The most important thing, I began repeating to myself like a mantra, was that we were going to be free. *Free!* I had not seen my family for almost a month. Finally, we would be reunited.

A few evenings later, I walked into my home. I was greeted by mustiness, mingled with the lavish scent of my father's pipe tobacco. The shades were drawn, the house was dark. My father sat mute at the edge of his bed, smoking his pipe, his face haggard and unshaven. His eyes looked at me blankly. The family's tower of strength now sat silent, beaten, and powerless, a wounded tiger in retreat. I wanted to say something to him, but my voice broke. I tried to swallow the sob in my throat.

My mother greeted me warmly, but her voice was grave, and her eyes welled with tears. Her dark hair was pulled tightly into a bun on the back of her head. "We can't open the windows," she cautioned me, "or in any way show that we live in the house. The man the mob left is still outside, watching us. You must walk and talk very quietly during the day. At night, the watchman is gone, and it's all right to make noise."

Nonno, my grandfather, put his shaking hand on my head, his voice breaking. As he sobbed, he blessed me by reciting a Hebrew prayer: *"Baruch atah athonai eloheinu melech ha'olam . . ."* This ritual, a symbol of his religious observance, reconnected me with my Jewish heritage.

Over the few days that followed, the family sat together around the table, but we did not touch the food. We walked noiselessly around the house. We did not speak much about our future. Stillness filled the warm, stuffy air. At times, the silence was so strong, I could hear it—the silence of fear. It slowly crept into my soul.

I spent many hours alone in my room, immersed in my thoughts. I felt as though my youth had been snatched away from me, ripped out of my hands and broken like fragile glass, shattering into pieces all around me. I wanted to scream with anger, but my screams never escaped the dark spot in my soul.

As much as my family and I wanted to leave the oppressive environment surrounding us, we recognized that our perpetrators would dictate the terms of our departure. We would be given no time to plan or make provisions for the future, a reality that caused in me a strange mix of feelings, from a sense of deprivation to one of relief.

A few days after my return home, a firm knock on the door broke the never-ending silence. Fearful, we didn't open it. Minutes later, however, we heard our neighbor's voice, "Open up, it's me." I opened the door.

Our neighbor was accompanied by a uniformed officer—a man in his forties, tall and broad-shouldered. He had olive skin, a thick-trimmed mustache, and jet-black hair that was greased with brilliantine. He wore a starched military khaki uniform and shiny, black leather boots, adding weight to his already-imposing figure. The colorful stripes adorning his lapel signaled his authority.

I glanced at the officer, taking in his stiffness, but when his expressionless eyes met my gaze, I lowered mine. He asked for my father. I stepped back, allowing him to enter our dark, musty living room. The officer told my family that if we wanted to leave the country, we needed to give him our travel documents. He would procure exit visas for us and return the documents in a few days.

My father went to the safe to get our travel documents. Jews were not allowed to have passports, because we were not recognized as citizens. Without proper passports, we were severely restricted from traveling outside of Libya. My father returned, holding the documents in his hand, a worried look on his face. He hesitated. *Didn't Deborah's family also surrender their identification papers to the police? Didn't the police tell them they were going to take the whole family to a military camp, for their own safety?*

As my father stood holding the documents in his hand, nobody spoke. After a few minutes, he handed over the documents and whispered to the officer, "Please follow me. I want to speak with you privately." The officer followed him to the living room, and my father closed the door behind them. Later on, my father told me about their conversation.

"I can make out a check for you," my father had said. "You can cash it today, in exchange for providing my family and me a police escort, to see us safely to the airport." The officer became excited. "Sure, sure," he replied, "you can count on me!" He left with the check in his hand.

A few days later, the officer returned with our visas. A month had passed since the Six-Day War, and Radio Cairo had reported Egypt's victory over Israel. Occasionally, my father was able to tune in to the BBC. The government jammed it constantly, but we were able to hear that Israel, in fact, had won the war and taken Jerusalem. We did not know what to believe.

In the midst of this confusion, we found out that the few planes leaving Tripoli were full, as a result of the panic the riots had created. Brian and Deidre came to the rescue, calling on their friendship with the British Airlines director. By taking off seven British passengers, the director was able to secure seven seats for my family. Destination: Malta, a small island and

British protectorate off the North African coast. We were finally leaving.

The night prior to our departure, I could not sleep, and I doubt anyone else could either. Pacing the floor, I could not make up my mind about what I wanted to pack. I was allowed only one bag. Should I just take clothes? What about my school diplomas and other mementos, which were so much a part of my life? And the photographs! I picked up my photo album and slid my fingers over its black-lacquered cover. It was hand-painted, with the image of Tripoli's castle in pale pink, a gray-blue mosque next to it, and a calm turquoise seascape with white surf hitting against the sea walls. "Souvenir of Libya" was painted in gold letters at the bottom. This serene cover was such an ironic contradiction to the political turbulence plaguing my country.

Leafing through my album, I saw photos of myself in boarding school in Switzerland, with my closest and dearest friends, and I saw photos of myself posing with my cousins at Giorginpopli Beach. The black-and-white photo brought back the summer days I had spent swimming in the warm water, eating yummy *panini be'tonno u felfel*—tuna sandwiches with hot peppers—that Nonna, my grandma, used to pack for me.

These photos were my memories, and I knew I had to take them with me. I walked toward my bag, took out my only winter sweater and replaced it with the photo album. Shortly after, my mother walked into my room and said, "Make sure you take some warm clothes with you." I nodded. I knew my friends and cousins would keep me warm.

At 5:00 A.M. the next morning, the doorbell rang. Two soldiers wearing fatigues and army boots stood at the door, with machine guns strapped around their shoulders. In a monotonous tone, one of them said, "We are taking you to the airport. We are the escort you asked for. *Yella*. Let's go." The soldiers ran downstairs to wait for us, their boots making a staccato sound as they moved with agility down the tiled stairs.

A military truck with another two soldiers waited outside our house. These soldiers greeted us with hostile silence and penetrating stares, and I was struck by the extent to which they were consumed by hatred. Were they really driving us to the airport, or were they driving us to our death?

The military truck drove only a few blocks, leaving us outside a hotel on the outskirts of town. The officer my father had bribed was waiting there. My father approached him. "Why are your soldiers not escorting us all the way to the airport?" my father asked. "Remember, you and I had a deal." The officer's face turned red, and his veins swelled at his temples. In a rage, he shouted, "Do you think that we have nothing better to do than to protect Jews? You want to go to the airport, take the bus!"

The officer boarded the military truck, where all the soldiers laughed and jeered at us, leaving us stranded on the street with our suitcases. Shortly after, an airport bus pulled up. As my family boarded, I noticed that the driver and the conductor (in charge of bus fare) were the only other people on the bus.

As soon as the bus took off, the conductor asked to see our passports and airline tickets. As his fingers slid across the pages of our documents, I whispered to my mother, "It's unusual for a bus conductor to check passports, don't you think?" She nodded. Something was not right, and I felt frightened.

I leaned my head against the cool glass window. In the airless heat, my throat felt dry; my head ached; and my hands were feverish. It was about six in the morning, and dawn was breaking, lighting up the sky. There were a few palm trees scattered along the arid landscape, and the silhouettes of a few laden donkeys appeared in the distance. Tin rooftops of scattered huts shimmered in the warm morning light as the town moved away from us.

Engrossed in the stillness of the landscape, I pondered the unpredictability of our future. From a distance, I heard the Muslim call to prayer, *Allah Akbar!* (G-d is great!) Suddenly, without warning, the bus stopped. I shot up out of my seat and walked to the front of the bus. "What's going on? Why did you stop?" I asked the conductor.

"There is something wrong with the engine," he answered. "I will have to go and call a taxi for you." He got off the bus and squatted down, looking under the engine. Drops of perspiration trickled down his nose. When I called down to ask if he knew what was wrong with the bus, he waved his arms around his head but remained silent.

The conductor returned to his seat, muttering, "There is something wrong, can't you see? There is something wrong." I turned to look at the rest of my family. Nonna Regina, my grandmother who was always in control, appeared anguished and fragile. Nonno, my grandfather, gave me a thin, bitter smile and continued to pray. My mother was pale, tears streaming down her cheeks. My father stared stonily out the window, as though to blot out any danger that might confront us. I felt my heart aching.

I approached the conductor. "If you get us to the airport, I will get my father to compensate you well," I said with a trembling voice. "We can make a deal."

"You Jewish whore!" he spat accusingly. "You are killing our brothers in Palestine!" His face was red, eyes intense with rage. He dismissed me by raising his arm toward me, then got off the bus and disappeared in the distance.

A knot grew in my throat. Where was he going? I turned to my mother and told her I was going to get help. I looked around furtively, then darted off the bus. As I ran, my stomach burned, and my legs quivered. My face and neck dripped with sweat. My fury kept me going.

From a distance, about half a mile away, I discerned a square, concrete building with men standing outside. I was passing by a *kahwa*, a roadside café, where men congregated, drank coffee, and smoked water pipes. Women were not permitted entry, as Muslim tradition strictly forbade them from being in the same room with men who were not close members of the family.

When I got close, I heard loud, excited voices fused with the Libyan national anthem, the "Jamahiriya," on a blaring radio. The men in the cafe stood at attention, bellowing, "*Ya biladi, Ya biladi . . .*" with passion and fervor. Suddenly, the singing stopped. The announcer introduced General Gamal Abdel Nasser, Egypt's president. As Nasser spoke, the excitement and anger surged, a fire fused with hatred. "We must free our brothers in Palestine . . ."

What if these men noticed me, a woman walking alone in a semi-deserted area at 6:00 A.M.? I could easily be killed or worse yet, raped. Perspiration soaked through my dress. My legs stiffened with fear, but the voices battling inside me slowly subsided. My courage was rekindled by the thought that my actions could affect the outcome of a whole lifetime for my family and myself.

I began walking gingerly, as though stepping on flowers, past the *kahwa*, looking straight ahead. I approached a gas station, and the pungent smell of gasoline invaded my nostrils. I asked the attendant if I could use the phone. He looked at me with curious eyes, then pointed to a small cabin. When I entered, I thought my heart would stop. The bus conductor was inside the cabin, using the phone. "Yes," I heard him say, "everything is under control." As he faced the small entrance, he saw me, and his face turned ashen. He hung up but kept his hand on the receiver.

"I need to use the phone," I said. Narrowing his eyebrows, the conductor gave me a stern look and kept his hand on the receiver. The room was small, dusty, and silent. A naked bulb hung on an old electric cord, gleaming a dim light.

I stood motionless, facing the conductor. I had no desire to look at his cold, questioning eyes. I simply wanted him to go away, to leave us alone. I prayed that he would not physically assault me, for I knew I would fight back, even if I had to pay with my life. My throat was tight, my eyes itchy, my head pounding.

I thought of the past few weeks, image after image burning in my mind. Our only way out was through a phone call. *I must seize that phone!*

I snatched the receiver from the conductor's hand, turned toward the wall to avoid his gaze, and dialed, calling Brian's English neighbor. "We are in danger," I said, speaking in English as fast as I could, for fear the conductor would understand what I was saying and sabotage my only escape plan. "We are on the road to the airport, about a kilometer away from the first gas station as you leave town. You must tell Brian. You must come quickly. We are in danger! We are in danger!" As soon as I heard, "We'll be there," I hung up.

I turned toward the door to leave, but three men blocked the exit—the conductor, the gas station attendant, and a third man. The conductor was in the middle. He stared at me. The air was thick, suffocating. There was a moment of stillness.

Freedom was on the other side of that doorway.

With a burst of energy, I pushed my way through the men and ran, noticing the expression of surprise and bewilderment as I passed. I ran and ran and ran. Although it took me about twenty minutes, it seemed as though I were running for hours. By the time I reached the bus, I was completely out of breath.

As I approached, the first thing I noticed was the driver standing near the bus. Trotting closer, I saw a pool of liquid beneath the vehicle—gasoline that the driver had discharged from the tank! I realized the plan was to set the bus on fire, and my heart hammered. My family was still inside, still silent.

The driver was holding something tightly—a box of matches. Fixing my eyes on the matchbox, I followed every move of the driver's hands. I looked back quickly, to see how far away the fast-approaching conductor was.

The conductor caught up with me at the bus, and he and the driver both stood facing me, staring, saying nothing. Peasants on donkeys and people on their way to work began congregating around, whispering to one another. One young boy pointed at the bus and shouted, *"Yehuda!* (Jews!)" As my gaze traveled from the matches in the conductor's hand to the road behind the bus, where I scoured the landscape for Brian's jeep, everything seemed to move very slowly.

Suddenly a jeep appeared on the horizon, followed by another jeep, and I began to sob. Brian and his friend raced up to the bus, saw the pool of gasoline, and motioned to me to get my family off immediately. Brian looked at the driver and said, "I am a mechanical engineer. Would you like me to look at the engine and tell you what is wrong?" The driver said, "No, no, we have called for help, thank you." Neither the driver nor the conductor tried to stop us. They just stared in disbelief, as my family quickly crammed into the two jeeps and sped off.

When we arrived at the airport, a young man asked to see our passports. He looked at our documents and exclaimed in disbelief, "Bublil family?! You are not supposed to be here!" If we had any doubts about a plot to kill us, they were promptly dispelled.

Customs officials handed us sheets and sheets of forms to fill out. My hands trembled, and I had such difficulty holding the pen; filling out the paperwork seemed to take forever.

Next, the porters refused to load our luggage onto the plane, because we were Jews and we therefore had to load our own bags. The officer in charge of passport control additionally commanded my father, "Hand over the keys to your car and tell me where it is parked. I have a big family, I need a big car." My father did as he was told.

Finally, we all boarded the plane. As the steward closed the plane door, I counted the members of my family. My uncle was missing. "Stop!" I yelled. I ran back to passport control, where my uncle was standing in the center of the room, encircled by porters and airport workers. They were spitting at him and waving their fists, laughing cruelly.

"We will kill you and cut you into pieces!" I heard someone shout. I grabbed my uncle's hand, cold with fear, and said, "Let's go! The plane is leaving!"

Forty-five minutes later, we landed in Malta. Forty-five minutes from oppression to freedom.

Nurses, doctors, and stretchers greeted us. The crew did not know what had happened to us before boarding the plane, but just by looking at our faces, they decided to radio in for an ambulance. Struggling through sobs, we tried to express our gratitude to the nurses and the plane crew. "Do you need help?" they asked. "What happened to you?"

"There are still Jews in Libya," my father cautioned us in

Arabic. "We can't say anything, or there may be retaliation." We all looked at each other and cried uncontrollably. My mouth felt dry. When I tried to ask the nurse for water, words would not come out; I felt as though I were being choked.

In Malta, we boarded a plane to Rome. After a short flight, we landed in the Italian capital. We saw a large, friendly crowd waiting for their relatives. They were waving their arms, talking and laughing. A handsome young man winked at me and with a dashing smile said, *"Ciao!"* Then I looked up and saw the most beautiful sight—a sign which said *Benvenuti a Roma!*

Vashti

When I was eleven years old, I went as Queen Esther to my Hebrew school's Purim carnival. As part of my costume, I wore a fancy, peach-satin dress and lots of makeup, like that of a grown woman. I still can recall how my mother applied it to my face: She piled on foundation because I had terrible acne. I hated its weight. Between every application, I put my head under a towel, over a bowl filled with steaming water. Doing so, my mother explained, helped the makeup settle on my face.

Next, my mother pinched my eyelashes between eyelash curlers, then proceeded to apply mascara to my naturally thick, long lashes. Then came the blush and the lipstick. For many girls that age, it was exciting to be allowed to wear makeup. I, on the other hand, was painfully aware that my mother was dressing me up not simply for the sake of my Purim costume; she had the greater purpose of making me appear beautiful to the entire community attending the carnival that day. She made this futile attempt in the hopes that those who met me would remember me as a pretty girl and make a mental note to seek me out in a few years when I would be of a marriageable age for their sons or nephews. That day was the first time I tried to look like Esther, but it certainly was not the first time I had encountered her.

Esther and her shadow have always been in Iranian Jewish women's lives. Around the world every year, it is customary for Jews to publicly read the Book of Esther on Purim—a holiday which celebrates the Jews' deliverance from destruction in the ancient Persian city of Shushan. The Book of Esther begins with King Ashasuerus throwing an extravagant banquet to show off the wealth and splendor of his Persian kingdom. While he entertains his nobles and governors, Queen Vashti, his wife, throws her own lavish banquet for women. From the outset, it is clear that Vashti sees herself as an equal.

The king's banquet is full of gaiety and celebration, until Vashti receives orders to come "before the king wearing a royal diadem, to display her beauty to the peoples and the officials; for she [is] a beautiful woman. But Queen Vashti refuse[s] to come at the king's command, conveyed by the eunuchs. The king [is] greatly incensed, and his fury burn[s] within him."[1] Vashti's act of disobedience and self-assertiveness is viewed as so powerful that the king's sages fear that "the queen's behavior will make all wives despise their husbands. . ."[2] Consequently, the king makes Vashti an example for all women in the kingdom, by banishing her from Persia: "All wives will treat their husbands with respect, high and low alike . . . Every man should wield authority in his home."[3]

At this point in the Book of Esther, Vashti is cast into the dark, the shadow. We never hear of her again. A classic interpretation of the text portrays her briefly mentioned character as villainous, the archetypal whore figure. She in fact is so hated that when the story is read publicly, the audience usually jeers upon hearing her name. A feminist reading, however, suggests that she is Betty De Shong Meador's definition of a "full woman," as "she gives up her favored status as . . . helpmate to her husband and stands in her stature and strength as a woman, restoring her identification . . . with women."[4]

Esther is the exact opposite. As the story continues, the king calls a search for "beautiful young virgins" throughout the kingdom, from which the king is to choose a new wife. A Jewish man named Mordechai enters Esther, his cousin and adopted daughter, into this beauty contest. Esther's obedience is noted soon after she appears in the story: "Esther did not reveal her people or her kindred, for Mordechai had told her not to reveal it."[5] The contrast between her and Vashti is immediately apparent. Not only do we see Esther in the role of classic virgin and obedient daughter, but we also find out that she is not pushy or assertive while in the palace, waiting to be seen by the king: "She did not ask for anything but what Hegai, the king's eunuch, guardian of the women, advised."[6]

Even after Esther becomes queen, she continues her "good girl" role. When the king's advisor, Haman, plans to destroy the Jews, Esther saves her people in a manipulative and passive manner. She does not confront her husband about Haman's plan or reveal that she too is a Jew and will be put to death. Instead, she fasts for three days and makes two feasts for the king, so that she may win his favor and reveal Haman's character to him indirectly.[7]

Esther has become the paragon of the good wife and the good Jewish woman. Many Jewish women in fact observe *Ta'anit Esther* (the Fast of Esther) on the day before Purim, to mark her importance. If she has acquired a kind of goddess status in the Jewish community, it is especially strong among Iranian Jews, where her Persian identity has sculpted her into the perfect role model for girls and women, including myself.

In the Book of Esther, Esther and Vashti never met. But growing up, I met both every day. The two were omnipresent archetypes in my childhood and adolescence, confronting each other in my daily life as a young, Iranian-born, American Jew.

Persians have a saying that follows every exciting event or accomplishment that involves children in their pre-marital life: *Enshala bara-ye aroosit.* (May the same happiness be for the time you are married.) I grew up resenting this so-called blessing, because it was a reminder of what was considered the essence of my existence—to become a wife. As far back as I can remember in my childhood, almost all of my behaviors, and my mother's influence on them, related to the day I would become a bride. My life became dichotomous, as my actions went into one of two categories—some would get me married (Esther), others formed strikes against me in finding the "right" husband (Vashti).

I remember being explicitly told as a child that expressing my anger or disappointment, especially in public, would decrease my chances of ever getting married. I also learned that asserting my desire, anything contrary to the script I was to follow, would transgress my marital path. I was an Esther-in-training.

Most significantly, the Esther/Vashti dichotomy strongly influenced my sexuality. The Persian Jewish dictum goes something like this: Persian girls must remain virgins until their wedding night. No exceptions. Do not wear tampons. Do not do splits in gymnastics. Do not ride a bike or a horse too roughly. Do not do *anything* to endanger breaking your hymen. Do not befriend boys. Do not even think about dating them.

Dating is perhaps the greatest prohibition in a Persian Jewish girl's teen years. It is something "others" do (or so parents think). The majority of Persian Jewish girls actually do date in high school, although at great risk. For this reason, lying becomes part of our repertoire of survival skills during adolescence.

The closest most girls in my age group came to openly dating was after high school, as they went on ritualized dates to determine marital compatibility. I was more fortunate than others. My parents allowed me to date after graduating from high school without the expectation that I would find a marriage partner in doing so. This small freedom, however, was kept a secret from most family members and the greater community.

This meant my boyfriend of four years, Gregg, who would later become my husband, was unable to share fully in my life. My parents feared how others would judge me if they knew I was dating. Given that Gregg is Ashkenazi, nobody could mistake him for one of my cousins; so my appearance with him would give away the fact that we were dating. The secrecy put a lot of strain on our relationship. If Gregg had not been as understanding as he was, I doubt we would be married today.

Keeping one of the most important relationships in my life a secret spoke of an even greater restriction that encompassed my entire life: Just like Esther, I hid my true identity, on many levels, to protect my place in the community. Vashti publicly declared who she was—a woman equal to her husband, not a toy for his and other men's amusement. But Vashti was condemned and excommunicated.

Just as Esther continued to be secretive and passive after marriage, to protect her life and status, so have Iranian Jewish women continued to hide behind a mask after their wedding days, to prevent alienation from their community. Like Esther, we are to be treated like queens in public—bejeweled and adored by our husbands. But also like Esther, we must know our place, or we will be "dethroned."

Generally, Iranian Jewish women do not share power equally in marriage. Often, age differences of nearly ten years preclude the women from any power at all. For this reason, many in my community are puzzled or amused by my egalitarian marriage, shocked to learn that my husband admires my feminism and identifies as pro-feminist himself. Our relationship may be novel in my community, but I would not have settled for anything less.

My mother once told me how commonplace it was for men and boys in Tehran to touch and grab at her, while passing on the street or standing on a crowded bus. I was shocked. I asked if she had yelled at the men or somehow made it clear that it was not okay for them to grab her. "A dignified woman would never draw that kind of attention to herself," my mother responded. "Only a whore would cause such a scene in public." A whore like Vashti.

Vashti never acted sexually in any way in the Book of Esther. She did, however, claim her right to her body. If a virtuous woman offers up her body to her husband, then what kind of a woman would assert her own rights to it?

Iranian Jewish women and girls still struggle with the shadow of Vashti—the authentic woman who wants to come out of hiding—the woman who owns her body, acts on her will, speaks her mind, risks it all; the woman who explores her body by herself and with others, when and as *she* chooses to do so. Numerous forces suppress Vashti deep inside ourselves. Sadly, the strongest of these forces is our mothers, who gag our sexual expression until our wedding nights, when men grant us permission to learn about our bodies; for just like Esther, we are supposed to take all our cues from the men.

Four years as a women's studies major have not erased all the programming I endured in the cult of Esther. The only reason I have the privilege to write about sex, and how Iranian Jewish girls must not even think about it before marriage, is that I am already married. Still, even though I am a wholehearted feminist, it is hard to get my words out, for even married women are not supposed to publicly share their ideas about sexuality.

As I write, I am aware that my thoughts may make powerful waves in the Iranian-American Jewish community. I know people may hate me and jeer at me, as with Vashti on Purim. The women in my community who wear Esther's mask may fear my words. But despite my own fears, I have unmasked myself and come out of Esther's oppressive shadow. From this place in my authentic self, I invite all of us to bring Vashti out of the shadow and into our hearts.

BENIGN IGNORANCE OR
PERSISTENT RESISTANCE?

●

I am an Iraqi-Egyptian Jew. When I asked my mother how long she thought the family lived in Iraq, she answered, "Probably since the Babylonian exile, over 2,500 years ago." My father was born and raised in Mansoura, Egypt. He told me our family, originally farmers in rural Egypt, farmed the land for countless generations in Moustawi. When they left for Mit Gharm, there were so many of us that the *fellahin*, the locals, referred to the place as *Kafr Wahba* (Wahba Village). His mother's side, more "recent" Egyptians, made the Sephardic journey from Spain to North Africa during the Spanish expulsion of 1492. They passed through Algeria, Morocco, Turkey, Syria, and Palestine, before finally settling in Egypt generations ago.

My parents chose exile over oppression, leaving Iraq and Egypt when Hitler was on the march. They knew there was "no future for Jews" in their native lands, and it was time to get out. My mother left Baghdad in 1943, two years after surviving the Farhud. My father said good-bye to "his" Egypt (he will always be an Egyptian) in 1939, after witnessing the growing popularity of Hitler's *Mein Kampf* translated into Arabic and sold in Cairo bookstores throughout the 1930s. "It was over for the Jews in Egypt," he told me, "even though we were there before the Arabs, before Islam."

I was born in India, where my parents met after leaving their respective countries. When I was three years old, my father moved to Osaka, Japan, for business. He left Bombay before us, on his soon-to-be-defunct Egyptian passport. The expectation was that my pregnant mother and I would follow as soon as the Egyptian consul procured the promised visa or *laisser-passer* (travel documents in lieu of a passport) from Egypt. We ended up waiting in Bombay for an entire year until the International Red Cross finally issued us the necessary travel documents.

Once my father left, my mother found herself facing a sexist and anti-Jewish bureaucratic nightmare, in which she was sent back and forth between government agencies. The Iraqi consul told her she was no longer Iraqi, since she had married an Egyptian. "Go to the Egyptian consul," he instructed. The Egyptian consul in turn told my mother she was ineligible for travel papers because she was a Jew. "Go back to your Iraqi consul," he dismissed her. "Soon no Jews will be Egyptian, not even your husband." While my mother ran from place to place, editorials in Egyptian papers called for a "pure" Egypt, with Jews—no matter how deeply rooted in Egypt—labeled "foreigners," foreshadowing the expulsion of Jews throughout North Africa and the Middle East.

In Bombay, my mother was left with nowhere to turn. She went to the Indian consulate, where she was informed that as a woman married to a foreigner, she could not apply for an Indian passport. The International Red Cross claimed my mother had left Iraq voluntarily, and since she was not a refugee in their eyes, they would not help her. To qualify for their aid, my mother had to prove that the Iraqi and Egyptian governments refused to give her papers. After much pleading, she got the Egyptian consul to document his refusal to issue her visa or any like documents. The International Red Cross finally recognized my mother's situation and issued the necessary travel papers.

With her now six-month-old baby and me, my mother finally flew out of India. Soon after our arrival in Japan, however, my father's passport expired, and we became officially stateless. For more than twenty years, my parents waited for U.S. immigration papers so they could emigrate to America. Ironically, the United States considered us Egyptian nationals, thereby making us vie for an almost nonexistent number of spots for Egyptians allowed into the country.

I managed to leave Japan before the rest of my family: My parents put me on a plane for Los Angeles as soon as I graduated from high school. I flew out with Red Cross papers again, this time with a student visa to attend college. I planned to study a little, within two years fall in love, marry, become a citizen, and bring my family over. Little did I know the United States would grant my parents citizenship only three years after my departure.

Like most other Diaspora Jews, my family considered the United States the only Jewish alternative to Israel. *Aliyah* was out of the question. Although most of our family did end up in Israel after they were forced out of Iraq and Egypt, my mother refused to return to the Middle East. Israel was badly situated, she said, too close to the nightmare she had escaped.

My mother was sixteen when the Farhud broke out. It was only luck that she lived on the outskirts of Baghdad, beyond the Jewish Quarter where the very poor Jews lived—the ones always hit the hardest. "The screams, the screams . . ." my mother recalled painfully. For two full days, Iraqi mobs unleashed rage upon Baghdad's traumatized Jews. "The noise was coming closer and closer, it went on and on . . ."

Jumping over rooftop terraces to a cousin's home farther away from the city, my mother fled with her family. After permitting mobs to assault Jews for forty-eight hours, the British finally deployed Iraqi troops to stop the rampage. When it was over, my mother saw the Tigris River filled with pieces of Jewish homes and lives—things the looters took but found no use for—floating down the river. For two weeks following the massacre, my mother slept with her shoes on, ready to run at a moment's notice.

After witnessing the horror—mothers and daughters raped in front of their families, babies pulled limb from limb, men slaughtered—my mother fled from Iraq. What she had seen altered her forever. "I will never live next door to the Arabs again," she vowed. "I got out of Iraq, and I am not going back." To feel safe, to be able to sleep at night, my mother had to be thousands of miles from the place she remembered with fear, far away from countries where Jews lived in terror. America represented a place where Jews had opportunity, freedom, and most importantly, safety.

When I arrived in the United States, my separation anxiety was masked by the almost unbearable excitement of finally being in America. I was overjoyed to be in California and to experience everything that came with it—including a huge community of Jews. The culture shock was exhilarating. In Kobe, I grew up knowing not only all the Jews, but all the foreigners. The fifty Jewish families that filled our small synagogue were just a tiny fraction of Kobe's non-Japanese population.

Many Jews throughout Japan were refugees—from Arab countries as well as from Holocaust Europe. We lived among the Japanese in varying degrees of separation, first as outsiders—as *gaijin* (pejorative for "foreigners")—and then as Jews among the *gaijin*. We were an extended family, an international tribe, one people with similar histories from different places.

I grew up feeling connected to all Jews in my community, so I was not prepared to be seen as "other" by Jews in Los Angeles. Suddenly people questioned whether I was "really Jewish" because I did not grow up eating bagels and cream cheese, or because my grandmother did not speak Yiddish. At best, I was marginalized and treated as exotic. At worst, I was made to feel invisible and irrelevant.

As it remains today, my primary identity back in 1964 was "Jew." Exacerbated by statelessness, "Jew" was also my nationality: I did not make *aliyah,* so I was not Israeli. I could never be a Japanese Jew, because assimilation was not an option—*gaijin* remained *gaijin*. And it would be a long time before I could call myself an American Jew. I was a Jew, period. All my other identities—woman, mother, daughter, grandmother, wife, partner, brown-skinned person, psychotherapist, feminist, heterosexual, lesbian—came second, in varying degrees and at different times over the years.

Originally, I thought, *Wow! Here I am in Los Angeles—a place filled with Jews just like me!* Most of the Jewish teens I met, however, were not at all "like me." They were second- and third-generation Ashkenazi Jews. The Persian Jews had not yet fled from Iran to Los Angeles. Had I arrived after Khomeini's ascent to power, the Jewish community would have looked very different. In the mid-sixties, though, American Jews were oblivious to the existence of Mizrahim and Sephardim.

Most of my new friends referred to themselves as Jew*ish*, and a number were uncomfortable with my excitement and identification as a "Jew." They were busy being Los Angeles teenagers, bleaching out the Jew in them, being cool. It was as if I were exposing something they were trying to assimilate out of.

They took for granted their huge synagogues, thriving Jewish community centers, summer camps, and schools with lots of other Jewish families and kids their age. To them, my unabashed excitement to connect as fellow Jews probably seemed odd, overdone, weird. We certainly did not take the same things for granted. I grew up in an international community, and I took *that* for granted. I grew up among Jews from Syria, Iraq, Iran, Poland, Russia, Panama . . . It was no different being a Moroccan Jew than being a German Jew. Everyone these kids knew, in contrast, was Ashkenazi.

The Middle East was not in the news the way it is today, so most of the people I met had never even heard of North African and Middle Eastern Jews. Every time I was invited for holidays, I found myself having to explain that yes, I was in fact a Jew, even though my parents were from Egypt and Iraq. *Even though?*

I also was approached endlessly with strange questions about where I got my enviable "tan." Admittedly, this take on my skin color was better for my self-esteem than my childhood experience of Japanese boys yelling, "*Curombo!* (Nigger!)" at me and my little brother, or overhearing people say how pretty I was, "but pity she's so dark."

In some of the more disturbing incidents, I found myself perceived as primitive and dangerous. My Ashkenazi-American roommate, Ellen, shared her mother's response to my background: "She told me, 'Watch out, those people can be very dirty,'" Ellen recounted. Ellen and I laughed about her mother's ignorance, but inside I felt a mix of shock, shame, and anger.

When my parents' American immigration number finally came up in 1969, my father was offered a job in San Francisco. It was easy to talk my then-husband into moving to the Bay Area with our baby daughter, to be closer to my parents.

My mother went to work for a jeweler she adored, an Eastern European immigrant. Their mutual respect and admiration was obvious, but this man could never quite understand how such a sophisticated person could have come from such a "backward culture." He repeatedly introduced my mother to people with a sensationalistic, "Can you believe it, she is Jewish and Arab! Unheard of!"

When I went back to college for my graduate studies in clinical social work, one of my professors was genuinely confused after I told him I was an Iraqi-Egyptian Jew. "So your parents came from Russia or Poland," he reasoned out loud, "and went to the Middle East from there?" I was stunned into speechlessness as I stood before this highly educated Jew who took pride in his social activism.

After graduating, I worked closely with a wonderful Ashkenazi psychoanalyst, many years my senior, and we connected deeply as fellow Jews and as immigrants. Precisely at those moments of connection, though, my colleague would look at me with a loving but puzzled expression and ask, "Ruchela"—a Yiddish twist on Rachel—"are you sure you don't know Yiddish?"

My colleague knew my history well. He loved his Eastern European heritage, but for some reason he could not incorporate my North African and Middle Eastern heritage into his own; it just did not feel Jewish to him. I wonder about an unconscious and deep-rooted need to identify as European. How does a politically conscious community continue to have such problems with Mizrahim, with Eastern Jews? Our experience is so consistently considered strange, inferior, or irrelevant, when in fact it is such an integral part of the Jewish story.

Kicked out of one country, invited into another, and cast away again, Jews have lived all around the world. But I find an unwillingness to stretch the Jewish net wide enough to acknowledge its diversity. So often, for example, when I correct people who speak of "Jewish" food and "the Jewish language" as exclusively European, these individuals respond defensively, as if I am taking something away from them.

What I want is inclusion, for all Jews to be an equal part, rather than to be subsumed into European Jewish culture or marginalized as exotic. I want more than being celebrated once every ten years at a "special" function.

I understand that "German Jew," "Polish Jew," and "Russian Jew" are terms familiar to Ashkenazi, evocative of where their home once was. "Iraqi Jew" and "Egyptian Jew" do not mirror the Ashkenazi experience or remind Ashkenazim of their past. But after I have just told my story, how can an intelligent person ask me, "Don't you miss hearing your *bubbe*'s Yiddish?"

I do see a change: People have more consciousness about the Middle East, and we are recognized much more today than when I first arrived in the United States. There remains resistance, however, to integrating the Mizrahi and Sephardi experiences, the multiculturalism of Jewish culture, into the totality of Jewishness.

On a personal level, what bothers me most is the loss within me. I find myself reacting badly to *Yiddishkeit;* sadly, it has come to symbolize invisibility and invalidation of my own heritage. I joke about having become "allergic" to Yiddish as a result. When I hear *Shabbat* pronounced *"Shabbes,"* for example, I cringe. I never had a problem with Yiddish before; I loved it as a vital part of our collective heritage—one of the many Jewish languages and cultures, an integral part of our incredibly textured history.

I no longer want to hold onto the anger, the defensiveness, the rejection, this alienating chip on my shoulder. *Gut Shabbes, Shebbath Shalom, Shabbat Shalom . . .* I want it all. Equally valid, equally unique, equally "Jewish." Unfortunately, the Jewish community does not seem to reflect my eagerness for embracing our diversity.

Not so long ago, for example, I enrolled in a class through Lehrhaus Judaica, a Jewish adult education institution in the Bay Area, called "The Jewish Life Cycle." As part of class, we were given a text, *The Lifetime of a Jew: Throughout the Ages of Jewish History.* This book, our only required reading, attempted to teach how to live life as a Jew, describing the customs and rituals of the Jewish life cycle. The book was exclusively Ashkenazi in assumption and form, with one exception: "A word should be said concerning the plan of transliteration followed in this book," the author noted in the introduction. "Usually schemes of transliteration follow the *S'fardic* pronunciation. In view of the fact that the Jews in America use mainly the *Ashk'nazic* pronunciation, many of the Hebrew terms when transliterated in accordance with *S'fardic* practice *strike them as strange. . . .*" (italics mine).

"Strike them as strange?" Since when is our way too strange for other Jews to relate? How alienating to have such attitudes prevail, serving to limit and disconnect Ashkenazi Jews from a vital part of their own Jewish culture.

In another class, "Jewish Spirtuality," the teacher stated that Jewish mysticism began with the Ba'al Shem Tov in Eastern Europe. I could not believe what I was hearing, and I waited for her to talk about the Sephardi mystics, who far predated the Ba'al Shem Tov. Not only did she not mention them, but she seemed completely uninterested in them.

I have even been asked if I can relate to the Holocaust. "What would you know? You're an Arab," a third-generation Ashkenazi-American friend threw at me sarcastically. Perhaps she made this statement to avoid a subject that always evokes pain. Unfortunately, it was at my expense.

I was in my early teens when I began reading about the Holocaust. Learning about it shattered my trust and broke my heart. I was in Catholic school at the time, where all foreigners were enrolled, and I chose to do my oral book report on this tragedy. I wanted my class to know what happened in Nazi Germany, since it was never mentioned in our studies, and I wanted everyone to care. To my shock and horror, the class responded to my report by agreeing that Hitler "built good roads in Germany" and that as a baptized Catholic, he would have eventually ended up in Heaven (after serving time in Purgatory, of course) if in his last moments he had repented sincerely. The unbaptized Jew, however—namely, me—would never reach Heaven.

I have always known that it was only circumstance that the Germans did not advance into all the Arab countries, which were eagerly waiting to deliver their Jews to the Germans for annihilation. Nazis wiped out the Sephardim, in Salonika and

Rhodes. In Tunisia, Nazis sent the Jews to slave labor camps. Nazi rule reached Iraq and was on its way in Egypt, but the Allies stopped it in both countries. My family was aware we were next. The grand mufti, Hajj Amin al-Husayni, was meeting with Hitler in Berlin, and as I mentioned, *Mein Kampf* was a bestseller in Egypt. "They were waiting," my mother told me. "We were on the list."

Sometimes when I bring up the oppression of Jews in Arab countries, progressive Jews get strangely uncomfortable—as if recognizing the Jewish experience under Islam would make someone racist and anti-Arab. During my mother's cancer support group intake, I listened as my mother told her story of living in Baghdad and surviving the Farhud. She ended with an ironic "I survived the Arabs to get cancer?" The Jewish oncology nurse was shocked that my mother was so "blunt."

Should we revise our history? Leave out the details of our oppression under Islam? Pretend my mother never saw the Shiite merchants in Karballah wash their hands after doing business with her father, because he was a "dirty Jew?"

I am constantly frustrated with the media as well, where the Jewish experience still continues to be defined as Ashkenazi. In news interviews with Israelis, Mizrahi and Sephardi Jews are rarely, if ever, mentioned. My father and I often talk about how amazed we are to see, over and over again, Israelis interviewed by American reporters on TV, with the reporters wanting to know how they "manage to rationalize living in a land that belonged to the Arabs."

In one such interview, an American reporter asked a Romanian-Israeli woman how she envisioned the new peace accord, whether she would be "willing to leave [her] settlement, should it come under Palestinian rule." The woman responded adamantly, saying she would never accept such a situation. Her reason? "The Arabs have the rest of the Middle East. . . . We lost everything. . . . Let the Arabs give us back our homes in Romania, in Hungary, all over Europe." I waited for her to go on, to speak about the 900,000 Jewish refugees from Iraq, Syria, Morocco, Egypt, Libya, Lebanon, Yemen . . . mostly absorbed by Israel. I waited for her to discuss how Arab Muslim governments took everything from these Jews and expelled us or forced us to flee from what had been our homes for thousands of years. But nothing. Not a word about that.

I watched and listened as the reporter continued to push the popular angle of how European Jews (i.e., Israelis) displaced indigenous people (i.e., Palestinians), and I imagined the reporter thinking, "What do the Arabs have to do with what Europe did to the Jews? Why do they have to pay for Europe's sins?"

We are the "other" indigenous Middle Eastern people who have been displaced. Why are we not part of the equation, in analyses and discussions of Arab-Israeli relations? Why has our historical-political experience hardly, if ever, been mentioned? And why have the Arab states never been held accountable for their actions against us?

I used to believe these attitudes were just the result of benign ignorance—a lack of education, exposure, and awareness that Jews are a multicultural people. I have come to feel, however, that these attitudes have more to do with outright denial, resistance, and fear in the Jewish mainstream—wanting to identify with the West, not wanting to be seen as "other."

Not only do Mizrahim and Sephardim face ignorance and resistance in the United States and other parts of the world, where we are a minority, but we also face these issues in Israel, where we have long been the majority of the Jewish population. During Israel's earlier years, Jews indigenous to North Africa and the Middle East streamed into the country. As we did, Ashkenazim approached us with prejudice and fear—fear of contamination, fear of making Israel a truly Middle Eastern nation. The Israeli (Ashkenazi) establishment did not hide its horror; the Levant was a filthy place from which dirty Jews from Muslim countries came. They would be taught European ways, for integrating these "backward" cultures was not in the plan.

The integration nonetheless was inevitable. While fraught with complexities, Jewish multiculturalism is alive and well in Israel today. Our parallel Ashkenazi and Mizrahi/Sephardi histories are intertwined; our people encompass Jews from Ethiopia, Mexico, and India; and our passions intersect.

It only makes sense to think of Jewish culture as the totality of the international Jewish experience, and for the various Jewish establishments to make it a priority to integrate all the diverse Jewish trajectories. I know it is going to take longer than I want for Jewish organizations to be more inclusive, expansive, and open to what is unfamiliar—seemingly "not Jewish"—but I am convinced it will happen. Narrow spaces open, creating opportunities for change as a result. I have seen it in my own family, and I have seen it in the Jewish community as a whole:

In the 1970s, when radical change was common, I left my husband and marriage of seven years, joined the counterculture, and expanded my mind. I went back to college, where I discovered the women's movement. Those were very important years for me, as I grew out of a mindset defined by sexism and fear. I realized I did not have to be married and tied to a man, that I could forge my own path (even though I had no clue what it meant at the time). I could do something my mother never had the opportunity to do—make choices that were about my own growth.

The umbrella of support for sexual openness flowed from the psychedelic enlightenment of the '60s and '70s, bringing with it a new consciousness that was expansive beyond anything I could imagine. Sexism and new openness brought me "out," and love keeps me "in" a lesbian relationship of twenty-five years, one that continues to grow and transform.

When I came out as a lesbian, my parents were enraged, afraid I would be thrown out of the Jewish world. There would never be room, they said, for gay people to be a part of Jewish life. They were convinced I was making a terrible, irrevocable mistake. "No, you cannot!" my mother screamed. "The Jewish people will never accept you. Since when do you make a 'choice' to be an outcast? You are destroying your family, killing your father! And what about your daughter?"

Once a very traditional girl from the Orient, I had made the choice to take feminism to its logical extension and be with a woman. Obviously bisexual on the Kinsey scale, I could make that choice. My mother simply couldn't understand why I would do it. For her, staying safe was central. As a Jewish girl walking down the streets of Baghdad, learning to be invisible defined her life. In her world, one did not make choices that highlighted difference—blending in was a matter of life and death. And here was her daughter, marching in the streets as an out lesbian! My mother was frightened.

What my parents predicted proved true to some extent;

there are groups in the Jewish world that have tried kicking me out. I remember when *Nice Jewish Girls: A Lesbian Anthology* was published. Evelyn Torton Beck, Melanie Kaye/Kantrowitz, Gloria Greenfield, Irena Klepfisz, Adrienne Rich, Savina Teubal (a Syrian-Argentinian Jew), and I gave a celebratory reading in Boston. Outside, the hall was picketed by a noisy group of Hassidic men in black coats, proclaiming our "excommunication." I thought, "Okay, it's a joke—a scary joke perhaps, but a joke nevertheless."

In Catholic school, I had learned about the power of the Vatican and the terror of excommunication. At home, my parents reassured me "once a Jew, always a Jew, no matter what." We do not have excommunication to worry about, they said. Before this demonstration, I had never met Jews who would consider such a thing. Perhaps these Hassidic men would have excommunicated my mother as well, because she began refusing to sit behind the curtain in the women's section of her synagogue.

As proud and passionate a Jew as she was, my mother also was deeply feminist. She no longer could tolerate what was intolerable—the "second-class status of women in this man-made religion," as she heatedly put it. She was no longer a second-class citizen as a Jew in Iraq, and she refused to be a second-class citizen in a synagogue.

So together, the women in my family started going to synagogue only once a year, on Yom Kippur, for *Neilah*. This practice evolved into our private custom, our bargain with God. After spending Yom Kippur day fasting and gently being at home together, Granny, Mom, my life partner Judy, my daughter Tiffany, and I went as a group to our Mizrahi/Sephardi synagogue. We arrived just in time to join in the spirited ancient chant, my mother's favorite passage, *"El nora Alilah, El nora Alilah, Hamsilanu Mehilah, Beshaath Ha Neilah . . ."* We were grateful for a way to connect to our heritage; and with our eyes closed and our hearts open, we could ignore the *mehisa* for a little while.

Dad, praying up front all day long, always knew when to stop and look back, beaming his loving smile at us. And so the High Holy Days would come to a close. Driving home, we anticipated breaking fast, the same way we did no matter where in the world we were: with hot black tea, cheese *sambousak*, *ba'aba* filled with mashed dates, *ka'ak* with its signature coriander, and Sara Lee pound cake (our more recent addition).

Before she died, my mother told me that my coming out as a lesbian was "the biggest trauma" of her life. I was shocked. "Worse than if I had become a nun?" I asked, sure she would say no. "Yes," she replied. "Worse than the Farhud?" Of course, she would say no to this. "Yes," she once again responded.

That did me in. I was ready to redo the past if I could. I lost all sense of what I had done for myself as being good and valid. I wished I had stayed the way I was and spared her the pain. I do not remember what I said exactly, but my mother interrupted me. "That was a long time ago," she said gently. "I don't feel that way anymore. I love Judy, you have to know that. I changed."

Change is never easy, but it is possible. What is most important to me is the willingness to change. On my end, I am willing to be patient.

In the more liberal sectors of the Jewish communities and synagogues, I have been delighted to find an incredible openness and movement towards acceptance and validation of lesbians and gays. Sexism and homophobia are being challenged in Reconstructionist and Reform Judaism, and such prejudice has been canonized as unacceptable in the newer Jewish Renewal movement. Changes are even happening in Conservative synagogues, though I still find myself frustrated.

I recently heard a *Shabbat* sermon by an inspired rabbi of a Conservative synagogue in San Francisco. He spoke of three necessary components for a good marriage: sexuality, friendship, and transcendence—the ability to transcend hurts and disappointments within a relationship. "We have that, Judy and I, exactly that," I thought, as I sat there listening. The rabbi, however, limited himself to referring only to "a man and a woman" in such unions. So many of us were experiencing good Jewish marriages, woman to woman and man to man. So many of us sitting right there, in this rabbi's congregation. The rabbi was aware of us. Was it politics that made him decide it was not time to confront this issue? Would he eventually consecrate gay unions? I know he has gay people in his life, whom he loves and accepts. Will he ever be able to deliver a relationship sermon that includes us?

When my mother died, my father went every morning to our Mizrahi/Sephardi synagogue, to say Kaddish. A year after my mother's death, my father and I went to this synagogue on a Sunday afternoon, for a presentation and workshop focusing on the plight of Syrian Jews. A dismal seven or so people showed up, for a slide show and letter-writing campaign, to help free this community in severe danger.

When the program was over, I spoke with the two very disappointed activists. In what I thought was a low enough voice, I suggested taking the presentation to Sha'ar Zahav—a gay synagogue, which boasts a large, socially active congregation. Hearing "Sha'ar Zahav," the rabbi flew from the back of the room into our faces and yelled, "Do not go to Sha'ar Zahav! Those people are not Jews. They are enemies of the Jewish people!" One of the young men gently stopped the rabbi from going any further.

The rabbi coincidentally then turned to me and said, "We love your father." They were so happy to have my father at services every day, with his beautiful voice and knowledge of the prayers. "We love your father!" the rabbi said again. I nodded, smiling; I also love my father. "Why don't you come too?" the rabbi invited. "Because I go to Sha'ar Zahav," I said evenly.

The rabbi froze. He just froze. And then he boomed in his big voice, "What are you doing with those people?"

"I am those people," I answered.

"No! I don't believe it!" he continued.

"Rabbi," I tried to explain, "'those people' are your children, doctors, lawyers, secretaries, and clerks. They are rich and poor. They are all of us, all Jews . . ."

I felt bad for my father. "I didn't mean to out you, Daddy," I said later in the car. "It's okay," he quietly reassured me. Such a different story now; I remember how my father fell into horror and shock when I first came out. But everything changes. "You grow with your children, or you lose them," my mother once told me when we talked about her coming to terms with my changes. As my mother grew and stretched beyond what was more traumatic for her than the Farhud, she grew to love my beloved, and to experience my relationship with Judy as a blessing.

And so it was that many years later, I found myself inadvertently outing my father in front of his rabbi. I liked the rabbi, and I knew my father had a good relationship with him. Although I felt bad, I had no regrets. As we drove off, my father reassured me that it was okay, that the rabbi probably was embarrassed but would get over it. "Prejudice only robs us of our humanity," my father continued. "There have always been gays in the synagogue. Only here in America, there can be a gay synagogue. I am sure we have gays in ours, too, but they just can't show it." When I first came out, my parents wished I would not talk about it.

When a community, a people, is gifted with diversity, we pay too high a price, suffer too much loss when we rigidly defend against embracing our differences. When we stop letting fear rob us of what belongs to us, we make the space for every Jew who cherishes identifying as a Jew. And we have more, not less.

I feel sad when I think of the rabbi casting out "those people"—those people who love their Judaism enough to create a safe synagogue. There are no "those people" within Judaism, be they in black hats and *sheidels* or hippie-inspired "rainbow" *tallits*, be they gay, bisexual, transgender, lesbian, or heterosexual, Ashkenazi, Mizrahi, Sephardi, or Ethiopian, women or men. The list is long. And no group needs to be "other." If we love our Judaism, our history, our culture, and our survival as Jews, we can open up the narrow spaces that harbor ignorance of how diverse a people we are. We can let go of the resistance to what on the surface fails to mirror our particular experience. It is enough that we are one people; we can reveal and support our different practices, shades, styles, and intensity.

I imagine the chip gone from my shoulder, the bitter taste of invisibility gone from my mouth. I long to let go of my own resistance, to identify once again with the totality of the Jewish experience. Writing this piece has healed the split in me. I feel my freedom to love Yiddish again, to wrap myself in our incredibly textured cultural tapestry, with all its diversity, depth, and brilliance. There is no acceptable alternative.

ELLA SHOHAT, MIRA ELIEZER,
AND TIKVA LEVY

BREAKING THE SILENCE[1]

$\mathcal{A}$t the Tenth National Feminist Conference in Israel, the brave women from HILA (Association for Education in the Poor Neighborhoods and Development Towns) raised a flag of rebellion: They asserted the need for frameworks separate from those of the current Israeli feminist movement and called for a separate national conference for Mizrahi women. For a number of years, HILA has helped Mizrahi women fight for equal rights for their children's education. This year was the first the organization had a leading role in preparing the national feminist conference and setting its agenda, creating panels and workshops to discuss the oppression of Mizrahi women and men.

HILA's strong roots in Mizrahi communities made it possible for the organization to motivate about two hundred Mizrahi women from the neighborhoods to come with their children to the conference. Harsh confrontations broke out between these women and the feminist leadership, confrontations similar to those that broke out in the late 1970s and the 1980s between Black women and the American feminist leadership. Mizrahi women challenged the hegemony of Ashkenazi women in their formulation of feminist theory, their attempts to silence Mizrahi women, and their attempts to distance from leadership Mizrahi feminists who would not accept the thinking and strategy postured by Ashkenazi feminists.

Ella Shohat
Good evening to everyone! *Masa il-hir. Ismi Ella, bass ismi il-asli Habiba. Hiyye Mira, bass isma il-asli Rima. U-hiyye Tikva, bass isma il-asli Amal.* For those who do not speak Arabic, I began my speech by presenting our current names—Ella, Mira, and Tikva—which were changed from our original names of Habiba, Rima, and Amal. Our Hebrew names were registered on our identity cards by our parents. They did not register our Arabic names.

In my case, I was named Habiba after my mother's grandmother, yet my mother did not register my name on my identity card. After her bitter experience with her own name, Aziza, she knew that in a society where our Arab names were associated with "the Arab enemy," in a society where anything related to the Middle East is considered inferior, constituting a stigma for one's entire life, in a society where an Arab name alone is likely to lead to shame and even failure, it was better to give a sabra-Hebrew name. Thus, our identity crisis as Mizrahi women begins already with our names.

Indeed, the matter of names is only one small component of our oppression. It nonetheless has symbolic value: Having been stamped with our sabra-Hebrew names, we learned it was wrong for us to live our culture in the present. We learned that we should erase our Mizrahi identity, so as to give birth to a sabra identity—namely, an Ashkenazi-Israeli identity.

Our mothers, in fact, whose names were changed by immigration clerks without so much as the wave of a hand, themselves continued the process which the establishment began: Having internalized the establishment's message that everything Mizrahi is disgusting, they gave us names which had no meaning for us. This gesture was an attempt to save us, their daughters, from shame and also an attempt to open the doors to success in Israeli society—doors locked for anyone identified with Mizrahi-ness. So consider the fact that a woman is embarrassed by her name. Her very name! *Kulitha shem!* All in all, it's just a name!

According to the hierarchies of racism and sexism in Israel, Ashkenazi women have enjoyed a higher social status than Mizrahi women, and we Mizrahi women have internalized the way we have been viewed. Even if we are politically active, even if we are aware of the discrimination Mizrahi Jews face in economics, politics, and education, it still is possible for us to be in an emotional-mental state in which we deny our Mizrahi identity. We still may be unable to liberate ourselves from Ashkenazi norms and expectations.

Growing up, we ordered our mothers to be quiet. In an attempt to climb the social ladder, we forbade them from speaking Arabic, Persian, Turkish, or Hindi. We pleaded with them to work on that Moroccan, Iraqi, or Yemenite accent of theirs when speaking Hebrew. We begged them to start being Israelis—in other words, Ashkenazi. Consider the fact that we, the girls, used our verbal power to censor and silence our mothers.

I see our struggle as Mizrahi feminists beginning first and foremost with our attempt to overcome external silencing mechanisms and our own self-silencing. As Mizrahi women, we are silenced both because of the institutional racism directed against Mizrahi Jews and because we live in a patriarchal society that oppresses women.

Given that we are standing at this intersection of several different forms of oppression, our struggle must be waged simultaneously on various fronts. These fronts include Mizrahi men who feel threatened by our feminist consciousness and Ashkenazi women who feel threatened by our Mizrahi identity. For us, there cannot be any separation between our battles in the different areas. Such separation would cause our struggle as Mizrahi feminists to fail.

A serious feminist struggle must be based on an in-depth analysis that examines the different contexts of our various forms of oppression. It must look at all of the circumstances at work in our lives as women. The struggle against oppression must be sensitive to these relationships and contexts, because the racism directed toward us is also a stumbling block in our lives as Mizrahi women.

The life of a young Ashkenazi student in north Tel Aviv, for example, whose father has a senior position in a company, university, or city council, is not the same as the life of a young Mizrahi student in south Tel Aviv, whose father is a factory worker. The Mizrahi student's chances of going very far are very slim. The Mizrahi student, worst of all, will internalize the oppression against her. She will come to believe that everything the East represents is negative. She will become convinced that being a secretary or hairdresser is the most she ever will be able to do.

In a world in which "the Oriental man is a wild beast, and the Oriental woman is to be enjoyed" (a Yiddish expression), the Mizrahi woman is perceived either as a wild, sexual animal or as a natural servant or housekeeper. It is true that all women are perceived as sexual objects. The stereotypes which are unique to us as Mizrahi women, however, further affect our place in this society and contribute to the difficulties that face us. Even in a society with equal rights for all women, we as Mizrahi women never will achieve the same as Ashkenazi women, as long as the media and educational system continue to teach us that Mizrahi Jews are inferior, backward, fanatical, and governed by uncontrollable impulses.

While Ashkenazi women more or less enjoy a continuity between their public and private cultures, we as Mizrahi women negotiate our way between different worlds. In our homes, for example, we continue to speak Arabic, Persian, Turkish, or Hebrew with a mixture of these languages. Mizrahi culture continues to influence our daily lives and behavior in an Ashkenazi-oriented society, yet we behave differently in this outer society than in our own Mizrahi society—particularly when we are in a group of Mizrahi feminist women.

During the last annual feminist conference in 1993, there was a drastic change: As a result of the insistence of Mizrahi feminists, we managed to achieve the principle of equal representation. The real feminist struggle and fruitful cooperation between women of different backgrounds, however, must be done on the basis of an additional principle: We must discuss and struggle against racism.

Every attempt to claim there is one feminist voice is an attempt to silence our own Mizrahi feminist voice. It is an attempt to dictate to us what is and is not important in our lives and which form our struggle should take. It is an attempt to direct us according to the Ashkenazi-feminist model. This model, however, does not work for us. Whereas the identity of Ashkenazi women is the unquestioned female norm and accepted as self-evident, our Mizrahi identity is under attack.

Through our discourse and struggle as Mizrahi feminists, we are dealing with our identity question. We are speaking according to *our* history and *our* current social circumstances. We are working to overcome our own self-silencing behavior, as well as the external attempts to silence us. Just by taking these steps, we *are* breaking the silence.

Mira Eliezer

Concerning this issue of silencing and internalization, I will focus on the area of education. In the audience, we have many mothers who have struggled to achieve a better education for their children. Two mothers here are part of the group of four Mizrahi mothers from Holon who petitioned the High Court of Justice for a better education for their children, by allowing the children to register in a good secondary school. The mothers won the case.

Every day at HILA (association for education in the poor neighborhoods and development towns), we hear innumerable examples of ways the educational system has tried to silence the mothers struggling against its discrimination. I went with one of the Mizrahi mothers in the audience, for example, to a meeting with a high-school headmaster, a guidance counselor, and a teacher. The headmaster turned to the mother and said in high Hebrew: "Mrs. Dorani, for what purpose did you initiate this meeting?" The mother turned to me and asked in Arabic what the man had said. I repeated the sentence in Hebrew, using a different tone, and what a wonder, Mrs. Dorani understood.

Another example, more pronounced, is a discussion between the supervisor of Jerusalem schools and a Mizrahi mother from the village of Ajour—a mother who also is in the audience. She tried to have her children registered in the Kibbutz Tsora'a school, which has a high level of education. She told the district supervisor that she wanted the children to get a high school certificate, so they could go to college. The district supervisor responded with an uproar of laughter.

Many women have been defeated when up against the open-fire of the educational establishment. When, however, we have come together in sisterhood on the basis of this common struggle, we have been more successful. Women who are united function as an integrated system, supporting one another.

The bombardment of Mizrahi women not only takes place when a Ministry of Education representative stands before a mother and says, "Nothing good is going to come of your daughter," a statement which is common. The bombardment also takes the form of general closed-heartedness and a lack of concern. Both stem from the belief that Mizrahi Jews are from a backward culture and society.

For example, I had a discussion with a guidance counselor from the Ministry of Education's open line for students. The advisor told me that HILA works with a weak population which maintains faith in such things as fate and G-d and which believes there is a hand which guides all things. Such a population, he said, is unable to take care of its own matters. According to him, HILA only incites this group to tackle problems which they are unable to deal with, because they do not have the capacity.

The educational establishment, composed primarily of women, treats mothers from poor neighborhoods and towns as if they were unable to raise and educate their own children. It sees them as being unable to discern what is best for their children and, thus, as being unable to take care of the children.

The situation was the same in the 1950s, following the mass immigration of Jews from Arab countries. Without consulting their respective parents, the government took children and dispersed them among educational institutions, according to party percentages. Many children were removed from their families and placed in boarding schools and kibbutzim, with the assumption that they would receive a better education. In boarding schools such as Aliyat-HaNoar, an educational project of the Jewish Agency, only seven percent of the students left with a high school certificate.

Today, the situation is the same with Ethiopian immigrants. In accordance with agreements signed between Aliyat-HaNoar and religious parties, the religious-vocational boarding schools have absorbed Ethiopian students, without consulting parents. The operating assumption is that Ethiopian parents are unable to take care of their own children; thus, the children must be removed from their families as early as possible. Authorities have not even bothered informing some parents about which boarding schools their children are attending.

Ethiopian parents explain that social workers even accompany the parents to their bedrooms and ask intimate questions, including those about sexual intercourse. They tell families how to dress and go so far as to open closets, throwing away clothing deemed "inappropriate." They tell mothers how to wash and feed their children. They instruct the children how to turn on bathroom faucets and how to use door handles. Social workers have gotten so involved, they have caused couples to divorce. Anyone who claims this situation existed long ago but not today should begin looking around. They should begin listening to what we have to say.

Tikva Levy

"Integration" is another aspect of oppression which is carried out by the educational system. In the name of "integration," the Mizrahi identity has been erased, and the Ashkenazi identity has been enforced. Boarding schools have been created for gifted children from families in need of "special attention"—read: Mizrahi families. The goal of these schools' founders has been to push the Mizrahi students intellectually into the Ashkenazi cultural patterns prevalent in our society. According to the founders, this goal can be achieved by creating among the Mizrahi students "a feeling of dissatisfaction with the existing situation, which can be generally referred to as a crisis. The assumption being that crisis is the precondition for the self-development and the realization of an ability to adapt to that world which is called 'Western' or 'modern' among those who were raised in cultural patterns referred to as 'Mizrahi' or 'traditional.'" These founders have seen the role of educators as being to participate in the developmental process of a Mizrahi student "in order to impart to the student a feeling of dissatisfaction with the existing situation and to increase her/his internal struggle until the student reaches a state of crisis."

Mizrahi students in these schools study with privileged Ashkenazi children. Nobody there ever speaks of the world the Mizrahi children have left behind. It is an intentional policy of silencing.

The message of those who implement these integration projects is two-fold: On one hand, it is "You are from a place not deserving of any attention," while on the other hand, it is "You are the chosen ones. All the others—your parents, your family, your friends—are worthless." The Mizrahi children express internalization of this oppression in various ways. One is by trying not to invite their parents to Parents' Day, so as not to be embarrassed by their parents' names, appearance, clothing, or even gestures such as hugging and kissing.

What happens to a young Mizrahi girl from such a school, when she comes home for vacation? Will she pretend she does not understand Arabic? Will she pretend she hates the Arabic or Mizrahi music to which her parents and friends in the neighborhood listen? Will she suddenly become a lover of classical (European) music? Will she bring her friends from school into the world from which she came? What is the price she will pay if she does or does not behave in each of these ways?

This crisis is exactly the kind which those in charge of the integration program have planned: a crisis in identity. Inherent in the integrationists' thinking is the assumption that such a crisis will lead to the creation of a new identity—an Ashkenazi-Israeli identity. The integrationists view themselves as revolutionaries, initiators of social change from which everyone will benefit. Their presupposition, of course, is that there is a superior Ashkenazi culture and an inferior Mizrahi one.

I see these "integrated" Mizrahi children as products of cultural oppression. I do not accept the explanation that shame of their parents' names, appearance, or language is the result of the generational gap. What is reflected here is a case of historical power relations between the weak and strong, between Ashkenazi and Mizrahi Jews.

As Mizrahi Jews, we have internalized the oppression so deeply that it is difficult for us to even imagine that we are able to destroy the model which Ashkenazi Jews have put before us, saying, "This is how you should be, otherwise, you are worthless." Which Mizrahi woman in the audience, after all, is able to imagine what it would be like to live in a society in which our dark color, our curly hair, and our Arabic names would be accepted as a given and as objects of worth in and of themselves? All of us here remember the times we ran to the hairdresser to straighten our hair. We all remember how every night before sleeping, we straightened it ourselves with some device, even an iron. From this reality alone, we can see just how oppressive a society can be. We can see how much this oppression can cause us to invest energy, time, money, and suffering just so that we can be similar, at least in our appearance, to the model which has been placed before us.

From here I would like to move on to another question: How many of us are trying to be accepted into a social clique or be active in a place with Ashkenazi hegemony—a place in which Ashkenazi Jews are in the positions of power? How many of us are active in societies or in organizations in which Mizrahi Jews set the tone?

This question leads me to examine the patterns of our activity as Mizrahi women in women's organizations. Given that I was one of this year's organizers of the conference, I had the opportunity to meet representatives from various feminist groups. My impression is that, in spite of all the posturing of openness and pluralism, Ashkenazi feminists still do not want Mizrahi women as partners. They do not want us to have power identical to theirs. They want to rule the feminist movement with the upper hand. From this year alone, my friends and I have a plethora of examples, but I will make do with only three:

First, in one of the preparatory meetings for this conference, a representative of Isha L'Isha (Woman to Woman, a feminist center in Haifa) announced to me that she had a message from a well-known feminist. It was a message, she said, with which she also agreed. The message was directed to the individuals who were planning to speak on "The History of My Oppression as a Mizrahi Woman." Blumenfeld asked that we focus on our oppression by Mizrahi men only, not on our oppression by Ashkenazi Jews, "to avoid creating conflicts in the conference." This request was an attempt to silence us.

Second, two weeks ago, the forum for preparing the conference convened to discuss the question, "How will we deal with the unintentional flood of Mizrahi women and their children, in terms of the budget and otherwise?" A representative from Shdulat Hanashim (The Women's Lobby) suggested we cancel the participation of Mizrahi women who had registered through HILA and, by way of compensation, organize for them another weekend with "two or three seminars on feminism."

Third, a few months ago, I attempted to create a broad front of women's organizations around the story of Karmela Buhbot. She is a Mizrahi woman from Kiryat Shmona who killed her husband after he had brutally and systematically beaten her for many years. I appealed to every women's organization I knew, with the suggestion that we launch a public campaign against the beating of women. I proposed that we place in the center the demand that Karmela Buhbot be put on trial for "manslaughter for self-defense," rather than murder.

The campaign was meant to be conducted the same way as the very successful campaign against rape, which was centered on the rape in Kibbutz Shomrat. In that case, a group of Ashkenazi youth repeatedly, for a number of days, raped a young girl from their kibbutz. Some organizations, such as the Tel Aviv branch of KLAF (the Lesbian Feminist Community), and A Home for Every Woman immediately responded positively. In contrast, after a week of negotiations, Shdulat Hanashim decided they were prepared to join the struggle only on the principle of battered women, but they refused to get into the specifics of the case of Karmela Buhbot. Why is it so obvious that we, as Mizrahi women, will join in a struggle against rape, when a kibbutznik Ashkenazi woman stands at the center of the struggle, while it is not at all obvious to Ashkenazi women that they need to support Karmela Buhbot from Kiryat Shmona?

Such examples and others lead me necessarily to the conclusion that for the time being, there can be no real, open, equal basis for cooperation between Mizrahi and Ashkenazi women in the various feminist organizations. From conversations with many Mizrahi women, the question arises: So what are we going to do? Should we remain active members in organizations controlled by Ashkenazi women and continue to suffer? Should we be content that we are given crumbs from the cake—such as a half-time position as a group moderator of Mizrahi women in the local neighborhood—and wave it around like a huge flag? Or should we say, "I no longer want to be the black square in a puzzle of white squares. I no longer will tolerate that on account of me, the organization receives large amounts of funds; while I remain outside the decision-making process. For this reason I am leaving. I will start to be active in those circles where I am accepted as an equal, directly into the centers of power, without any sort of entrance examinations. I will start to be active in places where I will be able to conduct matters without Ashkenazi paternalism, without limitations imposed onto me—limitations deriving from Ashkenazi fear that 'the day will come when Mizrahi women take the place of Ashkenazi women, in organizations which have been built by us.'"

Until the Eighth National Feminist Conference, there has been an absolute majority of Ashkenazi women—whether in conference organization, attendance, or content. Today, their status is beginning to be challenged, and the main proof is the quantity of Mizrahi women at this conference.

I want to conclude with a question for these Mizrahi women: Is there a place, not necessarily within this framework, to hold a conference for Mizrahi feminists, a conference in which the agenda will consist only of subjects and issues with which we deal on a daily basis? I know this question will cause a revolt among many women in the audience. These are the same women who will not hesitate for one second, to say yes when asked if there is a place for a feminist conference without men. I have been asked by many men and women whether it is not sexist to limit entrance to women only. My response has been, "It is enough for one man to be in a group of one hundred women to cause the women to shut up, to be silent, to feel shame and apologize when they say something against all men. We therefore need to give women a chance to meet alone." By the same token, I think that we—the Mizrahi women—need to be alone to clarify the questions and problems confronting us.

Ashkenazi women have had and continue to have opportunities to meet this way in the organizations controlled by them, and these kinds of meetings are indeed what they have had in the eight previous feminist conferences. We have jumped straight onto this cart, without any prior in-depth clarifying with ourselves of exactly to what we are aspiring; how we hope to achieve it; and how the history of our oppression as Mizrahi women enters into this whole process. It is time for us to begin clarifying.

ASHKENAZI EYES

W hen I was a child, I had a hard time saying I was American. If pressed, I said I was Californian. Los Angeles, where I grew up among diverse cultures, felt more accessible and familiar than the great expanse of America, with my images of Dick-and-Jane families who were far away from my frames of reference. My world was multicultural—from the intimacy of my home, shared with my Iraqi-Indian Jewish father and Russian-American Jewish mother, to our circles of friends, to my schools.

My Jewishness factored significantly into my struggle with claiming American identity. My neighbor, for example, regularly reminded me that I was not welcome in her house on Christmas Day, though she was happy to be my best friend the other 364 days a year. My early idealism also factored into the equation: Even at a young age, I was painfully aware that America had not lived up to its credos. I stopped saying "and justice for all" during the Pledge of Allegiance once I learned about the experience of African Americans.

Discussions with my immigrant father, who appreciated the freedoms he found in this country, forced me to question my distancing from American identity. As I learned about the history of activism in this country, I came to see that the very struggles to realize America's promise of democracy, liberty, and equality are in fact a quintessential part of what it means to be American. This perspective afforded me a window through which I might comfortably claim being American.

When I traveled to other parts of the world, I realized that I had no choice but to identify as American—both because of personal experiences of feeling foreign and because through the eyes of people of other nationalities, there was little chance I would be mistaken for anything but American.

Still, "American" continues to fall short of representing my cultural identity or even nationality. Even "American Jew" does not fully describe me, because the term conjures up images that reflect only half of me—bagels and lox, Woody Allen, the Holocaust, *yarmulkes,* and ancestors from Eastern European *shtetls.* People do not seem to realize that "American Jew" also means *chiturni* for dinner, a *hamsa* around the neck to ward off the Evil Eye, a henna party before marriage, and ancestors from Poona, India and Basra, Iraq.

I have hazel-green eyes—"Ashkenazi eyes," people tell me. These eyes and light skin conceal my Iraqi-Indian heritage, rendering half of me invisible. Before speaking with me about my experience or background, most people presume I am Jewish, and by that they mean Ashkenazi or white. Because I am especially close to my father's side of the family, it is difficult to have my ethnicity defined by others in a way that does not recognize my Mizrahi identity. People who are dark-skinned or still hold traces of an accent may tire of the question, "Where are you from?" But I would welcome the rare opportunity to round out people's perceptions of me.

Camp Shomria, New York, 1998
Kililili! Everyone clapped and shouted exuberantly upon hearing that three hundred people had made it to the reunion of our socialist-Zionist youth movement, where I had spent fourteen years of my life. I ululated, as is the custom among my dad's family when there is cause for celebration. *Kililili!* In response, one of the nearby ex-counselors raised his hands with two peace/victory signs and yelled, "Intifada!" An argument ensued, with several people contending that ululation was Palestinian, while I asserted that my style of ululation was Iraqi Jewish (and perhaps Iraqi in general). I was deeply disappointed by the exchange, feeling marginalized rather than embraced. Once again, I was invisible. My Ashkenazi friends seemed resistant to my assertion that Arab and Jewish culture are not necessarily polarized, but for many intertwined. I felt such tension, wondering if I was being too politically correct in the eyes of my peers. But having shared celebratory moments with both Palestinians and Iraqi Jews, I was confident in my assertion that the ululation styles were distinct.

My youth movement elicits a wealth of positive memories for me. I credit it with my early passion for social justice, as well as close friendships that continue today. Nonetheless, despite the fact that it was a Zionist organization with a focus on Israeli history, I learned next to nothing about the existence and immigration of Jews from Arab countries, let alone India. Over the years, as my family shared the history and culture of my Iraqi-Indian heritage, I developed a retrospective bitterness about the fact that American Jewish education teaches little or nothing about Mizrahim—in terms of our countries of origin, or in terms of the history of the state of Israel. My youth movement sent Israelis to America to support youth leadership and serve as educational resources about kibbutzim, democratic socialism, Zionism, and modern-day Israel. Thinking back, it is hard to believe they were able to talk about modern day Israel without discussing the Mizrahim, who for decades comprised the majority of Israel's Jewish population.

Ululating was my small attempt to bring my Mizrahi identity into a space so pivotal in my life and yet so deficient in teaching me critical information about my Jewish self. Despite the absence of education about non-Ashkenazi culture, I still had hoped I could make my heritage visible and accepted. But these "progressive" individuals mocked and rebuffed my action as non-Jewish, sending a message that there was no room for a Mizrahi girl to be her Mizrahi self in a leftist American Jewish organization.

On the flip side, a number of my Ashkenazi friends enjoyed the warmth and laughter of my father's extended family and were supportive of my forays into this side of my heritage. In addition, my Ashkenazi mother found a home among my dad's family and embraced Mizrahi culture; so at least in my immediate family, I never questioned the richness and value of either heritage.

Los Angeles, California:

Growing up American Jewish, Growing up Ashkenazi

My father was born in Poona. His father had immigrated to India from Iraq at the age of sixteen. His mother's family had lived in India for two generations, also after emigrating from Iraq. My last name, Iny (E'nee), has its origins in Ana, a predominantly Jewish town in ancient Babylon. My mother, on the other hand, is the granddaughter of immigrants from Odessa, Ukraine—for many years a vibrant center of Jewish life in Eastern Europe. The intensification of anti-Semitism, culminating in a series of pogroms, provoked their decision to migrate, first to Canada and then to St. Louis.

My brother and I are the mixed-heritage products of my parents' encounter, made possible by several twists of fate—a flood in Poona and my Indian grandparents' hospitality to an Ashkenazi geography professor from Missouri. My father, the only member of his family of six to attend university, was thwarted in his third year of studies when a torrential monsoon flood caused the town's dam to break. The lowlands of the campus site were so severely damaged that the school was closed indefinitely.

Meanwhile, my grandparents' home on Mahatma Gandhi Road was renowned for warm hospitality. The family opened their doors and hearts to friends, family, and innumerable travelers my grandfather met at the jeep repair and service shop where he worked as general manager.

Put the two together, and the result is a Jewish professor from Missouri who met and encouraged my father to apply to the University of Missouri in order to finish his degree. My father applied, received a scholarship, and went off to middle America when he was eighteen. The rest, as they say, is history.

My Indian grandparents did not know what to make of an American Jewish daughter-in-law. *Would she have loose morals like the women in the movies? Would she keep Georgie in America?* My American grandparents were worried about an Indian Jewish son-in-law who planned on returning home after university. *I don't want my daughter moving to Timbuktu.* Both sides actively discouraged their children from marrying.

Fortunately, my parents prevailed, and I was born into a loving family in 1972 in Los Angeles.

Growing up an American Jew, participating in mainstream Jewish organizations, I learned how to be Ashkenazi. I learned that Jews spoke Yiddish and drank Manischewitz, and I learned that the center of Jewish culture and persecution was in Europe. At home, where Jewish holidays are celebrated, most of our festivities followed Ashkenazi traditions, perhaps because of the proximity of my mom's side of the family.

Nonetheless, despite the geographic distance of my dad's family—scattered through England, Israel, and Canada—my brother and I developed strong emotional connections with several generations of cousins, aunts, and uncles on that side. Through these relationships and the culinary efforts of both my mom and dad, Iraqi-Indian Jewish culture found its way into my life.

Poona in the Mix:
A Typical Second-Generation American Experience
Indian food was central to my family's diet, both at home and at restaurants which we visited as soon as they opened. My mom remembers me begging to be taken to eat somewhere "normal" like other American kids. Visits from my granny or aunts offered the promise of potato chops (potato patties filled with meat or curried vegetables and accompanied by a cilantro chutney), *ba'ba* (date cookies), and *sambousak* (savory cheese pastries). My favorite childhood lullaby was in Hindi. Despite my mostly secular upbringing, Judeo-Arabic blessings peppered my vocabulary, and we held tightly to religious rituals believed to safeguard each other's well-being, such as throwing water after the footsteps of a person embarking on a journey.

When I was four, I offended an older Indian woman in a Los Angeles park when I fell from the swings and muttered what I thought was an innocuous Hindi expression of frustration. My dad, with his mischievous sense of humor, had taught it to us, confident that no one else would understand, as the Indian population was small in those days. But this woman gasped, not knowing what to think of a little white girl saying "mother-fucker" in Hindi, under her breath.

Only as an adult did I begin to decipher my vocabulary and pinpoint the cultural sources of my family's customs. A few years ago, for example, I found a cookbook on Indian Jewish cooking that centered on the Iraqi-Indian community, so I finally was able to determine whether my family's dishes were Indian or Iraqi in origin. Often, I found, they were a hybrid of both, perhaps retaining the Arabic name for a dish flavored with green chilies and other Indian spices.

Fortunately, I was able to spend time with my father's mother before she died in 1997. My granny, generous with equal-opportunity love, allowed each child, grandchild, and great-grandchild to feel a deep and special connection with her. She was the beloved matriarch; and after leaving Poona when my grandfather died in 1967, she became a mobile homeland, the focal point for the ingathering of her children in exile. She is the most visceral link I have to my Iraqi-Indian heritage, inspiring my attraction to Middle Eastern and Indian culture and motivating my desire to explore and express those parts of me.

I am still in the midst of this effort, begun in my early twenties, to learn more about my heritage—getting recipes and cooking lessons from my Aunt Rachel in Montreal, interviewing relatives about their lives in India, and occasionally foraying into Mizrahi synagogues. I did a brief stint as a singer for a Berkeley band singing Ladino and Mizrahi tunes; and while the experience of being a female singer without formal training in an all-male band was mixed, I am deeply grateful to have learned a few more prayers and songs that connect me to my people.

In my attempts to pinpoint the Iraqi-Indian influences in my life, it seems most difficult to convey to others what is perhaps at the core of my Mizrahi identity. The intangible— the warmth and joy of an Iny gathering, the generosity modeled by my dad and his siblings, the sheer love of being with family. In the community strongholds of my relatives, there was much Iraqi-Indian Jewish culture available to me with minimal searching. Outside those pockets, however, I was not raised in an Arab- or Indian-Jewish community. While there were Iraqi and even Iraqi-Indian Jews in Los Angeles, our connections were not strong, perhaps because of how spread out the community was.

My exploration into the Iraqi-Indian part of my identity was challenging not just for want of community, but because of assumptions that I was 100 percent Ashkenazi—assumptions that persisted even after I revealed my background. It was tiring to insist that people see past my complexion; it was easier to blend in and not make waves. Often, the more I asserted the Mizrahi side of my dual heritage, the more I felt vulnerable and isolated.

Part of my vulnerability came from a feeling that I did not seem to belong anywhere on the ethnicity map. With Ashkenazim, I lost my Arab-Jewish self; with Indians, I was embraced by some and treated indifferently or as a curiosity by others; with Arabs, I was "other" as a Jew, and with people of color, including some Mizrahim, my light skin privilege made me white. In addition, revealing my heritage occasionally made me privy to anti-Arab racism.

Today I struggle with the thought that people will view my emphasis on my Iraqi-Indian heritage as opportunistic, because in leftist circles I am more legitimate if I claim otherness. I silence myself, out of fear that people will belittle my thirst for information and understanding. They may see my light skin or ignorance of my heritage as a reason to find me disingenuous in wanting to learn more about my roots. Given all these forces, and given my fear that I cannot adequately represent what it means to be an Iraqi-Indian Jew anyhow, why take the risk of publicly claiming my identity?

Navigating Multiculturalism

As an undergraduate at U.C. Berkeley in the early 1990s, and in my current work building a multiracial alliance for social justice, I have found it necessary to define my own ethnicity and place myself in the multicultural landscape. Because I am both Mizrahi and Ashkenazi, I have found it particularly challenging to adopt existing terminology. There is widespread ignorance about Arab Jews; Conventional wisdom maintains that Jews are white, while Arabs are people of color.

In the many circles where people define community based on white and of-color categories, I thus feel utterly confused and homeless. People have suggested that if I have experienced racism, I am of color. But what if I have experienced racism in Israel and white privilege in the United States? I read essays that describe Arab Jews as Jews of color, but still I feel confused. If I am light-skinned, am I of color? What if I am light, but others in my family are dark?

I remember looking at my grandfather in his wedding

picture. *He looks Palestinian,* I thought. I felt pride. Palestinians were legitimate Arabs. My reaction indicates how absurd ethnic identity had become by the 1990s. The Palestinian litmus test I applied to my grandfather's picture testifies to the difficulty I experienced in trying to find my place in the modern multicultural paradigm.

Progressive circles claim that the Jewish experience is white, so I try to act responsibly and claim my white privilege. But that erases significant parts of my identity, experience, and culture.

My struggle with the politics of language makes me wonder who bequeaths identities. I would like to find those people; maybe they can help me figure out where a light-skinned, mixed-heritage, 100 percent Jewish girl belongs. I have some questions for them:

I want to know if Arabs with Crusader-blue eyes and light skin are still Arabs and still people of color.

I want to know what makes me different from light-skinned, second-generation immigrants from other communities of color. Should they call themselves white if they experience white privilege? If they do not speak the language of their grandparents or parents, and thus lack significant access to their heritage, do they lose "color points?"

I want to know if the term "of color" necessarily correlates with disadvantage. American Mizrahim experience the cultural discrimination, but not the systematic socioeconomic discrimination, perpetrated against Mizrahim in Israel. Who is more legitimately of color—a dark-skinned, middle-class, American Mizrahi from the suburbs, or a light-skinned, working-class, Israeli Mizrahi from a development town, Israel's equivalent to the inner city? If being "of color" correlates with discrimination based on obvious physical difference, then am I a person of color not because I am Iraqi-Indian, but simply because I am a Jew?

My most significant experiences of persecution had more to do with anti-Semitism than racism against Mizrahim. In my West Los Angeles junior high school, for example, I was ostracized and taunted because of my "big Jew nose," despite the large Jewish student population. My mom encouraged me to confront the anti-Semitism, which left me even more isolated when I found only one friend willing to be a public ally. After a year of public humiliation and oppression, this little Jewish girl hated to look at herself in the mirror and asked to change her nose. (Of course it was only because my family was middle class that I was able to come up with this "solution" to the oppression.) My parents, resistant to the idea, made sure that the doctor knew that I was Jewish and told him not to make any radical changes.

Looking back, I feel tenderness toward that little girl and the decision she made, but at the same time I feel shame. And then frustration: There was no language, no public discourse to foster pride and acceptance of my Jewish body. Little Jewish girls like me, harassed because of our Semitic features, were—and still are—forced to seek individual relief rather than communal support.

While I find all of these questions compelling in the landscape of discussions around multiculturalism, I also find myself stepping outside this paradigm and seeing something absurd about the minutiae occupying so much emotional and intellectual energy for me and other mixed-race, Jewish, or other borderline white folks. My experience reveals the limitations of the existing categories, as my identity is fluid, depending on where I am and what color line is in operation.

In Israel and in the American Jewish community, I am a person of color. In the broader context of United States racial dynamics, I am white. While identity politics may have the adverse effect of inhibiting inter-ethnic connections, I nonetheless believe they have the positive effect of raising consciousness and questions regarding what it might mean to foster truly inclusive, egalitarian communities.

White = Human; Ashkenazi = Jewish:
Privilege in the American Jewish Community

Antiracism activists maintain that it is precisely because of white privilege that many white people in the United States perceive white as normative and therefore do not consciously think of themselves as white each day, often identifying instead as "human" or simply "American." When people's heritage and faces are reflected in communal institutions and popular culture, the world is theirs, and a great deal more comfortable. Only when white people acknowledge their whiteness can they begin to critically assess the culture, examine the institutions and communities in their lives, and notice who is missing. This act of recognition can then inspire the next step of seeking to understand why their life, workplace, or neighborhood is so homogeneously white and to understand the role of personal and institutional racism in creating that situation.

In a similar dynamic, Ashkenazi Jews are able to attend "Jewish" events and belong to "Jewish" institutions, without seeing it as problematic that the culture and leaders are exclusively Ashkenazi. A few years ago I attended a Jewish meditation conference where over fifteen rabbis and lay leaders shared a diversity of meditation traditions. As a newcomer to Jewish meditation, I assumed the absence of Mizrahi leadership and tradition reflected the absence of meditation in that culture. I learned later that I was wrong.

If the organizers of this conference had acknowledged their Ashkenazi orientation, they might have sought out Mizrahi rabbis or lay leaders to teach Mizrahi meditation traditions. At least they might have publicly acknowledged the unfortunate homogeneity of the presenters, thus raising consciousness about the diversity of Jews in our community. As someone seeking to deepen my spiritual practice and cultural understanding, I look forward to a time of this kind of consciousness, so that children and adults with Jewish heritage from Iran, Ethiopia, India, Morocco, and Greece all will be able to learn about their own traditions from "Jewish" institutions.

I myself can feel comfortable in Ashkenazi settings. I share that heritage; and growing up in the United States, I have learned to equate communal Judaism with Ashkenazi culture, relegating my Iraqi-Indian culture to a familial context. This comfort makes it extremely challenging for me to think about confronting assumptions around what constitutes American Judaism. Who will be my ally? Will anyone back me up? I question my ability to play a role in educating Jewish leaders. As the Jewish meditation conference experience revealed, I do not even know what history I do not know; so how can I be an educator?

At Home in a Foreign Land:
My Time in Israel

I traveled to Israel for a year after high school, as part of a program for youth movement leaders. The trip catalyzed my interest in re-examining my cultural identity and analyzing the social forces that had caused me to identify predominantly as Ashkenazi. In the United States, Arab Jews are all but invisible;

there were few contexts for me to express my Iraqi heritage and receive recognition that my people existed. In Israel, not only does one find distinct communities of Yemenite, Libyan, and Iraqi Jews, but Ashkenazi cultural, political, and economic dominance over Arab Jews is a recognized phenomenon.

I had the opportunity to get close to my Iraqi family in Israel—aunts, uncles, and cousins of all ages who had made their way from Iraq, India, and Iran. Whenever possible, I spent weekends with my cousin, Susie, lying in her bed and talking about our lives. Though I was eighteen and she twenty-six, she treated me like a peer and became something like a sister to me—giving me hand-me-down clothes and open-hearted, non-judgmental support.

For the first time, I began to develop a communal identity, a connection with other Jews from the Middle East and North Africa, who were mostly thrilled to learn that I had Iraqi heritage. One Tunisian friend told me that she knew that I was "different." It was powerful to feel embraced and reflected by other Arab Jews who were not family members.

My identification was not seamless, however. As an American in Israel, I was perceived by many as quintessentially Western and therefore Ashkenazi. Moreover, I had to navigate the class differences between my middle-class self and the predominantly working-class Arab Jews. When I did my shopping in the crowded Souk Hacarmel, an outdoor market in Tel Aviv, where the majority of vendors are Arab Jews, I felt a connection with the vendors singing about their beautiful grapefruits. At the same time, I feared that this connection would not be reciprocated because I was American, and therefore moneyed. I wondered whether they could see me as one of their own, given our class differences.

I noticed similarities between the class/race dynamics I experienced in Israel and those impacting people of color in the United States. First, I had fears that as a middle-class individual, I was not authentically Mizrahi. Those fears were similar to the feelings expressed by some of my middle-class African-American friends, who received messages that to be authentically Black or "down," they had to be working class.

Second, as a light-skinned Mizrahi, I was an active witness to anti-Mizrahi racism. It was clear that I, like some culturally assimilated people of color in the United States, appeared "safe" enough for whites—in my case, Ashkenazi Israelis—to share with me their racist views about people with whom I shared an ethnic bond. It is perhaps because we are both able to "pass" and are members of the target group that people feel particularly drawn to confessing their prejudice.

Third, it seemed to me that working-class Mizrahi-Israelis, like young men of color in the United States, are under greater scrutiny regarding their materialism and sexuality than are members of their respective dominant cultures. For example, the pejorative word *arsim,* used to describe men who wear heavy gold jewelry, seem consumption-oriented, and are overtly sexual, is applied almost exclusively to Arab-Jewish men. So I was particularly pained when my progressive Ashkenazi friends insisted that *arsim,* unlike its predecessor *chah'chahim,*[1] was race-neutral. I was also troubled by the blatant classism in this practice of judging one group for its status displays, when such behavior can be found amongst people of all economic backgrounds. Nonetheless, when I tried speaking with Ashkenazi friends about these issues, they responded as if I was making a big deal out of nothing.

Shade in Israel:

Funny, You Don't Look Like an Iraqi-Indian-Ukrainian-American Jew

On a flight to Tel Aviv when I was a young adult, I connected with an attractive Israeli guy, and we went on a date upon our arrival. From the moment we were on the ground, I found myself carrying the burden of the conversation. Given that *he* had pursued *me*, I found the dynamic especially irritating. Toward the end of the evening, he finally began to engage me in conversation.

"Where did you grow up?" he asked.

"Los Angeles."

"Where are your parents from?"

"My mom is from Missouri, and my dad is from India."

"Indiana?"

"Lo, Hodu," I said. (No, India.)

I replied in Hebrew, so it would sink in. He offered me an incredulous look in response, so I explained (as I often do) that my father is Iraqi in origin. With a cliché intro, "I'm not racist, my best friend's Moroccan," he proceeded to explain to me that Mizrahim teach their kids to emphasize material success, whereas Ashkenazim teach their kids simply to be good people. Moreover, Mizrahim and Arabs have no problem lying. They are much more violent, and they are prone to incest. Mizrahim are also racist and more extreme than Ashkenazim, tending to vote overwhelmingly for Likud and Tzomet (right-wing Israeli parties). His family, in contrast, was from Czechoslovakia, and it was no coincidence that Bohemia was in that country, given the intellectual capacity of its citizens.

Within seconds, I felt paralyzed and disembodied. I felt violated, having shared physical intimacy with this racist jerk. All I could muster was to say that my dad's family included the most generous and loving people I knew. I could not access my anger, even as the idiot replied that my father's family most likely was influenced by the "nonviolent culture" of India—the Hindus, of course, being nonviolent, as opposed to the inherently violent Muslims.

Everything felt surreal. The racism was so blatant and unabashed, it seemed to have been scripted for a TV show. There I was with a man who was attracted to me because of my hazel-green eyes and light skin, which did not reveal my Mizrahi heritage. I assume he continued to see me as essentially Ashkenazi even after I had revealed my family background, given that he felt so comfortable spewing his vitriol at me. Precisely because the Arab Jew in me is often invisible to the naked eye, I was granted the opportunity to share an intimate moment with a man who loathed half of my being.

As such, while my experience in Israel fostered connections to Mizrahi communities, it also thrust Ashkenazi-centrism and racism vividly in my face. The awareness of Arab Jews and Jews from other non-European backgrounds did not seem to quell the urgent desire exhibited by many of my Ashkenazi-Israeli friends to simplify the complexity of my identity. American Jew = Ashkenazi. Period.

Since I lacked the requisite dark skin and eyes, they frowned upon my interest in broadening my experience of Arab-Jewish culture and tradition. Take Yom Kippur, 1996. "Why," an Ashkenazi friend asked in some mix of shock and horror, "would you want to go to a Mizrahi synagogue?" Rather than encourage me to reconnect the dots that had been systematically erased by my secular Ashkenazi upbringing, she reinforced the notion that there was nothing worthwhile to be found in a Mizrahi religious experience. Shamed, I did not go to the synagogue. Instead, I remained indoors, ironically breaking my fast with the Moroccan couscous her mother cooked. Mizrahi *food*, of course, is worthy of Ashkenazi affection.

What's Left:
Racism and Politics in Israel

In 1994 I went back to Israel to make tangible contributions toward advancing justice for Palestinians. The parties on the Left seemed to be doing the most in this regard in the political arena, so I spent eight months working and volunteering in a left-wing political party. I also volunteered for a Jewish-Palestinian organization that worked on reducing economic inequality among Israeli-Palestinians.[2]

Unfortunately, since Israel's inception, Ashkenazim have dominated the Left. Few Mizrahim/Sephardim will forget the Left's responsibility for spraying DDT on Mizrahim/Sephardim upon their arrival from North Africa and the Middle East. Few will forget these parties sending Mizrahim/Sephardim to marginal areas designated for "Eastern immigrants," areas which have become Israel's most poverty-stricken Jewish communities. Menachem Begin and the right-wing Likud party came to power in 1977 precisely because Mizrahim/Sephardim voted out the left-wing party responsible for their mistreatment.

I believe the left-wing Israeli parties offer the greatest promise of justice for Palestinians and civil and economic rights for all of Israel. If the Left wants to diversify and gain Mizrahi, Sephardi, Ethiopian, and Israeli-Palestinian support, however, they must acknowledge past and ongoing discrimination. Until they start understanding rather than diminishing the anger and pain of these communities, they will have little success wooing those voters.

Many of the left-wing Ashkenazim I have met outright deny the persistence of institutional and individual racism that welcomed Arab Jews upon arrival in "the Promised Land." When I highlight current disparities in income, education, and access to power, they kindly remind me that things have changed and that I am an American, anyhow (and therefore less entitled to describe what I see). Prior to Israel's election of Ehud Barak, I read an article in the *San Francisco Chronicle* that named his apparent weakness as candidate for prime minister: He greatly angered the Ashkenazi community by apologizing to the Mizrahim for the role Labor took in exacerbating social and economic inequality.

As long as denial is more powerful than empathy, Ashkenazi Jews will continue to have a hard time understanding Shas' (the predominantly working-class Mizrahi/Sephardi religious party) expanded representation in the Knesset as more than a religious phenomenon. They will be blind to their own racism, encoded in the hundreds of thousands of e-mailed pleas to former Prime Minister Barak when he was building his governing coalition: *Rak lo Shas.* (Just not Shas.)

Acknowledging racism and discrimination can be uncomfortable and awkward, but clearly it is the first step toward building a shared identity. Candor, education, value for and preservation of diverse cultures, and social and economic reparation must happen if Israel is to heal from its legacy of racism.

It's Not My Revolution If You Won't Dance at My Henna Party[3]
I love the richness of both sides of my heritage. I savor each new connection, each new morsel of knowledge that strengthens my relationship with the Mizrahi community and with my own family's traditions. But I have grander visions of

public victories: I have visions of genuine multicultural consciousness in the Jewish community's understanding of itself
and its history; visions of people no longer seeing the term
"Arab Jew" as an oxymoron, but rather as a promise of what
might happen in the Middle East if a just peace supersedes eth-
nocentrism; visions of my half-Iraqi cousin from a kibbutz
dancing at my henna party, not embarrassed by the expression
of Mizrahi culture and Arab music; visions of Israelis initiating
candid discussions among Palestinians, Mizrahim, Sephardim,
Ethiopians, and Ashkenazim, regarding how to promote social
justice and end racism.

I want to see the same institutional commitment to preserving
Judeo-Arabic and Ladino as there is to preserving Yiddish; to see
Jews throughout the world learning about and preserving Jewish
history in countries where there is but a smattering of Jews. I
want to visit Iraq, the country where my ancestors lived for thousands of years. I want to arrive as an "out" Iraqi-American Jewish
woman and visit Basra, the city my grandfather grew up in;
Baghdad, a center of Jewish culture and community; and Ana,
the town that is the root of my name.

Insh'allah. G-d willing.

YAEL ARAMI

A SYNAGOGUE OF ONE'S OWN

I was born in Petah Tikva, to parents who had arrived from Yemen in the great airlift of 1949. My grandparents all were religious, and they fastidiously kept the commandments in the traditional Yemenite way. My grandfathers would get up at the crack of dawn, praying and studying Mishna and Tehilim before a day of hard physical labor. In the afternoon they would say their Minha prayers and again study the Talmud. Their education was not Western or secular, but religious.

This same beautiful Yemenite tradition also dictated that my grandmothers were not to be educated at all. Indeed, neither of them ever learned to read or write in any language. I, however, attended state religious schools—public schools affiliated with the "knitted kippot" stream, i.e., the National Religious Party. I had a good experience in both junior high and high school; were it not for the encouragement I received there, I would not have become the first member of my extended family to graduate from university. In fact, I am convinced that had I been sent to one of the *moshav* schools attended by my cousins, I would not have done nearly as well academically.

And yet, although a significant number of the students at these schools were Mizrahi, prayers were conducted using an Ashkenazi prayer book and singing Ashkenazi melodies. The Jewish history curriculum consisted almost exclusively of Ashkenazi history. In many ways my junior high and high schools were a product of the comfortable, Ashkenazi-Orthodox bourgeoisie from which the National Religious Party has historically drawn its support. The schools were not a paradise of ethnic integration.

In junior high school, for example, the participants in the extracurricular program for "gifted" girls were overwhelmingly Ashkenazi. I could not help but notice that an Ashkenazi from a "good family" who received an average grade of seventy would be placed in the regular academic stream, while a Mizrahi with the same grade would be placed in the vocational stream.

Once, upon hearing that I would be taking high-level matriculation exams in biology and English, an Ashkenazi girl from an ultra-Orthodox Hassidic family—someone I knew from outside Yeshurun—expressed her honest surprise: "I thought Mizrahim didn't have the mental capacity to study subjects like that!"

As a small child, my Yemenite identity, my dark skin, my "different" religious traditions and culture, and my family's often difficult economic circumstances exercised few apparent effects on my life. The situation, however, changed greatly when I reached my teen years. Like almost everyone I knew from school, I became a member of Bnei Akiva, the National Religious Party's youth movement, where it soon became apparent that my "different" Yemenite features were not seen as beautiful. Suddenly, differences of ethnicity, skin color, culture, and class mattered greatly.

This dynamic was especially prevalent when it came to inter-actions with boys—about whom my friends and I knew pre-cious little, having attended single-sex schools all our lives. In high school, some of my Ashkenazi schoolmates declared, with the naïveté and candid honesty that young teenagers quickly outgrow, that they would never consider marrying a Mizrahi. Somehow, this determination that they not "intermarry"—that is, marry anyone who resembled the male members of my family—in no way prevented them from being good friends with my sister and me.

This same confused honesty came into play when another friend, sharing her adolescent angst, complained to me that because of her looks, people often made the terrible mistake of assuming that she was—G-d forbid!—Sephardi. She accepted without question the assumption that Sephardim (in Israel usually a synonym for Mizrahim) are inferior socially as well as mentally; that this claim was merely a fact of nature; and that the painful reality facing Sephardim would have had nothing whatsoever to do with her, were it not for the wretched misfortune of some people's classifica-tion error.

When I reached my late teens, the age at which it was deemed appropriate to begin helping me find a husband, people always matched me up with someone considered "suitable"—which invariably meant Yemenite or some other flavor of Mizrahi, but never, ever, Ashkenazi. I myself was more concerned with a potential partner's personality and intellect, regardless of his eth-nicity. Shortly before I married my husband—an American who moved to Israel as a teenager—a neighbor winked and said to me, *"Sichaqt otah!* (You really pulled off a good one, bagging yourself an American!)" As if marrying a Yemenite like myself would have been a lesser social achievement. If I *sichaqti otah*ed, what had Daniel done?

Israelis' almost instinctual desire to classify everyone according to ethnic background works in other, often bizarre, ways as well: Because my mother is not especially dark, and my sisters and I are relatively light-skinned, people frequently assume that only one of my parents is Yemenite. Moreover, when these individuals raise the matter, proud of their astuteness in the field of ethnoracial classification, they expect me to take their remark as a compliment!

In addition, upon hearing that I am a Yemenite, people frequently refuse to believe me, exclaiming—as they re-examine my nose and my curls—"But you don't look Yemenite!" This kind of remark also may be intended as some sort of compliment; but it is really a *complaint* that by looking the way I do, I am breaking the rules. After all, Yemenites should look like Yemenites, and we all know how Yemenites are supposed to look! Rather than recognize the absurdity of such physiognomic stereotypes (Yemenite Jews are, physiologically, an extremely diverse group), some people find it easier to reclassify me, going so far as to tell me to my face what I am and am not.

In Europe, my obviously non-European looks have resulted in some uncomfortable situations: In Germany, I have had to avoid certain areas, fearing local skinheads' reaction to my skin color. In France, I have been verbally ridiculed and insulted for being yet another ignorant North African who does not know French. In California, people's best intentions have resulted in a number of social blunders: When I left a tip in a San Francisco café, I got a courteous *"gracias"* from the politically correct Anglo waiter. After a predominantly African-American gospel group sang at a Marin County synagogue, several members of the congregation approached me, to express their admiration for our wonderful gospel performance! It seems that wherever I go in white-majority countries, I am, in accordance with local stereotypes, seen as the generic woman of color—Algerian in France, African American or Puerto Rican in California . . .

As I was growing up, the aspects of day-to-day life that had the most influence on my Yemenite identity were weddings, henna ceremonies (held before weddings), and, most importantly, the synagogue that I attended every *Shabbat* evening and morning, beginning at the age of five or six. At this synagogue, I picked up the traditional Yemenite melodies that dance through my head to this day. These melodies are so central not only to my identity, but also to the religious experience of praying, that when I regularly attend a synagogue in which the liturgy and the melodies are Ashkenazi, I sometimes feel as if I am in *galut* (exile).

Unfortunately, religious Mizrahi women, including myself, find ourselves in a trap. In Orthodox synagogues we are, as women, exiled as passive observers to the *ezrat nashim* (women's section), which is usually in the balcony. We are thus far removed from the liturgical action, which takes place in the middle of the men's section. We have heard the ancient melodies countless times and are familiar with every note and inflection. Yet when we decide not just to listen passively but to sing the prayers ourselves (perhaps just to ourselves, since some Orthodox men consider women's voices raised in song to be an abomination), we discover that we have been left mute, for only the boys have been sent to the *mori* (Yemenite religious teacher) to learn the liturgy and the tropes.

Another factor that has left countless Yemenite women unable to participate in Jewish life is their lack of a formal education—

Jewish or otherwise. Growing up, I often came across Yemenite women who could neither read nor write. I encountered many more who were able to read perfectly well but could not follow the prayers in the *siddur* (prayer book), because it contained abbreviations and shortcuts that only those initiated into the liturgy's many secrets—the men—were able to interpret and follow.

I myself learned to pray at school, and though I learned to pray in the Ashkenazi version of the liturgy, I soon found myself able to follow prayers unique to the Yemenite *Baladi* tradition. The Jews of Yemen have two principal liturgical traditions—the *Shami*, based on the Sephardi traditions of the land of Israel, and the *Baladi*, the local Yemenite liturgy that predates the *Shami*. Thanks to the background I received at school, I was able to help the other women in the balcony follow the prayers being read out down below. On an unofficial, volunteer basis I even taught a number of women from my synagogue to use the prayer book themselves.

The women's balcony proved a good place to learn about the circumstances under which the Yemenite women of Petah Tikva lived. Most women did not come with their families to synagogue, as the community discouraged women's participation—as if a praying wife was simply a wife who was not preparing a tasty meal. One woman actually had to physically elude her husband in order to come to the synagogue and pray silently. I should emphasize that such cases were relatively uncommon, but they did exist and formed part of the cultural landscape in which I grew up. In any case, the majority of women did not attend the synagogue at all, and in elementary school I was the only girl, other than my sister, who attended regularly.

As I neared high school age, though, more and more women—including teenagers—started coming to Shabbat services, a fortuitous consequence of the Ashkenazi "knitted kippot" norms then influencing Mizrahi society. I couldn't help notice that people sometimes left in the middle of the Shabbat morning prayers. For Yemenites, prayers start at 6:00 A.M. and are especially long, including a translation of the entire Torah portion into Aramaic. The men, it was clear, left because they were tired, whereas the women who slipped out did so to prepare salads and set the table for a meal.

In my family, both nuclear and extended, our role as women was fulfilled primarily by doing housework and preparing food for everyone. This value system was especially in evidence during the seven days of mourning, when the women were expected to prepare food for the family and the people who dropped by to express condolences and join in prayers. The women internalized this code of feminine behavior and were proud of playing their assigned roles, even secretly competing with each other to see who was fulfilling her role most successfully. When a man, as a joke, offered to help the women with their tasks, he was expelled from the kitchen with smiles and loud laughter all around. What man could possibly be serious about taking on the role of a woman?

This division of labor reached its peak during the holidays, especially *Sukkot* and Pesah. At *Sukkot,* the men built the *sukkah* (with so much construction talent in our family, doing so was never much of a problem). The women prepared vast quantities of food for the members of the extended family, who would be coming for the holiday feasts. Preparing the traditional dishes, however, was only the first part of the job; the second was to serve the food, carrying course after course out to the *sukkah,* and to cater to every whim of the men, who of course, never left their seats.

I remember an incident that took place when I was in sixth or seventh grade. The family was seated in the *sukkah,* and my uncle was ordering the women back and forth, demanding that they bring him salt or some dish. I was so busy catering to his needs that I hardly managed to partake in the meal. At some point, I'd had enough and simply refused to continue back and forth to serve him. "Praised be G-d!" I told him, "for He has endowed you, too, with two arms and two legs so that you can get up yourself and bring to the table whatever you desire!"

My uncle, angry at having his authority questioned, tried to re-establish his prerogative with a bit of disingenuous logic. "You're seated near the exit to the *sukkah,*" he countered, "and are thus closer to the house." He was right, of course. The woman had been intentionally seated near the exit, to facilitate their functioning as waitresses to the men. "All right," I said, "then let's change places." Tempers flared, and my mother hung her head in embarrassment—her "poorly brought-up and disrespectful" daughters had shamed her yet again.

Only the men actually slept in the *sukkah,* following one of the principal practices of *Sukkot,* because religious law has seen fit to exempt women from such onerous commandments. Indeed, there is no more effective a way to exclude women from participation in important religious ceremonies than to invoke the Talmudic ruling that women are exempted from carrying out *mitzvot she-hazman garman* (commandments that take time to perform), time that men thought Jewish women could better spend on housework, cooking, and taking care of the children.

At the end of *Sukkot,* on Simhat Torah—the holiday that

marks both the end and the beginning of the annual cycle of weekly Torah readings—the denizens of the balcony once again were excluded from the action at the synagogue. Unlike the men, the women were not allowed to dance with the sacred Torah scrolls, for at least two reasons—women were generally forbidden from dancing in view of men, and it was seen as inconceivable that women, made "unclean" by menstruation, should even touch the Holy Book.

In the Talmud, it is expressly written that Torah scrolls cannot contract impurity by touching objects or people believed to be impure. What's more, the Torah tells the story of Miriam, who does not ask for permission to dance after crossing the Red Sea out of Egypt. She grabs a drum and gathers the women around her. They dance and sing together. Traditions that help establish male privilege and women's exclusion nonetheless are always useful to the patriarchy and can acquire the force of law, even when they contradict the written law in both spirit and letter.

Pesah was the holiday during which I most keenly felt the injustice of traditional gender roles. The women worked for a full month before the holiday, cleaning every nook and cranny of the house to make it kosher for Passover and then cooking copious quantities of food, only to fall asleep at the Seder table from sheer exhaustion.

As early as sixth grade, I began to ask questions about the status of women in Judaism. The responses I received from teachers and rabbis ranged from straight-out justifications of the status quo, including a spirited defense of traditional women's roles, to the old canard that rather than discriminating against women, Judaism sees women as more exalted than men and thus requires that they perform fewer *mitzvot* (commandments). I really and truly wanted to believe those explanations, but at some point such casuistry ceased to be intellectually convincing.

I am well aware that traditional Jewish law, as it has been interpreted over the ages and as it affects Jewish women of all ethnicities, is full of provisions that sanctify inequalities between the sexes. Examples are legion, so I will mention just three particularly sensitive ones: Women cannot be counted as part of a *minyan* (the quorum of ten necessary to perform certain synagogue rituals); the barring of women as witnesses on certain matters in a court of law; and the inability of a woman to grant a *get* (writ of divorce) to her husband, despite the ruling of Rabeinu Gershom (tenth century)—and thus leading to pre-divorce blackmail ("I'll grant you a *get* and give you your life back if you sign over the house, the car, the dog. . . .").

In many cases Jewish tradition, as recorded in the Talmud and other texts, presents a broad spectrum of opinion on matters such as these. Indeed, the rabbis of old often argued with each other forcefully—the entire Talmud consists of such disputations—defending conflicting interpretations and sometimes coming to diametrically opposed conclusions. Unfortunately, in most Orthodox circles, the trend since the eighteenth century has been to choose the stricter, more oppressive option at every juncture regarding matters of women's rights and other areas of life.

For example, in the Mishna (Sota 3, 4), two conflicting opinions about educating girls are expressed. The first, that of Eliezer Ben Horkenos (a sage of the Shamai school), declares that "he who teaches Torah to his daughter, it is as if he teaches her foolishness." The second opinion, that of Shimon

Ben Azai (a sage who was a student of Rabbi Akiva), states simply that "a father is required to teach his daughter Torah." Unfortunately, these days few ultra-Orthodox Jews are familiar with Shimon Ben Azai's injunction. Instead, the leering contempt of Eliezer Ben Horkenos gets lots of airtime, and the Talmudically ignorant—who are legion among both the Orthodox and the ultra-Orthodox—treat his declaration as reflecting the true spirit of Jewish law.

In the works of Halacha (Jewish law) that have been compiled over the centuries, there arise numerous questions of when and where, and with which blessings, the *tallit* (prayer shawl) may be worn by women. Most authorities agree that women are permitted to wear a *tallit*, but they differ on whether a women is allowed to recite the blessing *"l'hit'atef batzitzit"* before donning the shawl. The lines in this dispute happen to divide Ashkenazi commentators from their Mizrahi and Sephardi counterparts, with the former allowing women to recite the blessing and the latter forbidding them to do so. Today, Orthodox rabbis from both communities are delegitimizing women's right to wear *tallit* at all.

If one examines how Halacha regarding women has developed over the centuries, evolving with the changing circumstances in which Jews live, it is clear that it was the rabbinic elites and Jewish society at large who chose to enshrine a segregatory approach to women despite the existence, within Halacha, of other options. In our time, as religious women are becoming more educated in reading and interpreting ancient Jewish texts as well as secular, modern ones, the time has come to re-examine the process by which the discriminatory and segregationist approach to women has come to dominate modern perceptions of Jewish law.

Certain segments of modern Orthodox Judaism have, in recent years, begun to undergo a quiet and limited transformation that reflects a certain awareness of feminist discourse. Women in some especially liberal institutions are being taught the Talmud, but I believe that Judaism must go much farther than even the most liberal, feminist-inspired fringes of modern Orthodox Judaism are, at present, willing to go, to achieve full equality for women in all matters, including synagogue ceremonies.

There needs to be exegetical, interpretive, and *psika* writing by women on the Torah, the Talmud, and Halacha in general that reflects a new spirit—one unconstrained by the interests of the male elites that, over the centuries, have edited and canonized Judaism's central texts. Giving women the right to learn the Talmud without permitting us to rule on it as well is like showing women the apple without allowing us to take a bite from it.

There must be women rabbis called *rabbot,* in the singular *rabba,* with all the functions and authority that male rabbis have. Women must have true positions of synagogue and community leadership. Once we attain these positions of power, we must remember other groups currently without voice in the Jewish community—including lesbians and gays, the mentally ill, and the disabled.

In a number of Orthodox circles, women may appear to have gained a certain level of progress: *To'anot rabaniot* (rabbinical pleaders) present women's divorce cases before rabbinical courts. These courts, however, are all male and do not even accept women as witnesses on certain matters. Female "Halacha counselors" are trained and certified by rabbis. But the rabbis are all men, and the counselors only may advise women on limited "female" aspects of Jewish law, such as *nida* (ritual impurity caused by menstruation) and *tahara* (purification by going to the *mikva* (ritual bath). As far as I am concerned, such "concessions" to feminism by the Orthodox establishment are the moral equivalent of forbidding women from driving cars and then letting a few select women play with the windshield wipers.

I do not deny that there are signs of some progress, but movement by Orthodox Judaism towards something resembling equality has been far too slow. Indeed, I have lost faith that the Orthodox leadership in Israel is capable of making the necessary changes in our lifetimes. Consequently, those of us who believe that Judaism must be egalitarian need not sit around and wait for the go-ahead from the Orthodox rabbinical establishment. We need to take a fresh look at Halacha—including the Talmud—ourselves; and where age-old texts do not provide the answers, we must not fear to create and to change within the framework of Halacha, just as Judaism's religious leadership has done for the past 3,000 years.

For instance, Shimon Ben Shetah, the Talmudic sage who drafted the *ketubah* (the traditional Jewish marriage contract, which grants a woman certain rights in case of divorce), initiated changes in marriage law because he saw a need to protect women from callous husbands. Today, injustices against women must be handled with similar Halachic verve and imagination.

I continue *lishmor mitzvot* (to keep the commandments), with one exception: I also have taken on traditionally men-only *mitzvot* which women are exempted, or in some cases even forbidden, from performing. My feminist world view, which has grown out of my experiences as a Yemenite woman, is thus now integrated into the way I lead my day-to-day ritual and spiritual life.

REFLECTIONS OF AN ARAB JEW

●

I am an Iraqi-Israeli woman living, writing, and teaching in the United States. Most members of my family were born and raised in Baghdad and now live in Iraq, Israel, the United States, England, and Holland.

When my grandmother first encountered Israeli society in the 1950s, she was convinced that the people who looked, spoke, and ate so differently—the Ashkenazi Jews—actually were European Christians. Jewishness for her generation was inextricably associated with a Middle Eastern identity. My grandmother, who still lives in Israel and communicates largely in Arabic, had to be taught to speak of "us" as Jews and "them" as Arabs. For those of us from the Middle East and North Africa, the operating distinctions had always been "Muslim," "Jew," and "Christian," not Arab versus Jew. For us, the assumption was that "Arabness" referred to a commonly shared culture and language, albeit one with religious differences.

Most Americans are amazed to discover the existentially nauseating or charmingly exotic possibilities of such a syncretic identity. I recall a well-established colleague who, despite my elaborate lessons on the history of Arab Jews, still had trouble understanding that I was not a tragic anomaly—the daughter of an Arab (Palestinian) and an Israeli (European Jew). I have found that living in North America makes it even more difficult to communicate that we are Jews entitled to our North African/Middle Eastern difference and that we are Arabs entitled to our religious difference (like Arab Christians and Arab Muslims)—all at the same time.

The policing of cultural borders in Israel led some Arab Jews to escape into the metropolises of syncretic identities. In the United States, we face again a hegemony that allows us to narrate only a single Jewish memory—a European one. For those of us who do not hide our North African/Middle Eastern-ness under one European-Jewish "we," it becomes more and more difficult to exist in an American context that is hostile to the very notion of Eastern-ness.

As an Arab Jew, I often am obliged to explain the "mysteries" of what people perceive as oxymoronic realities: Our communities traditionally spoke Judeo-Arabic, not Yiddish; for millennia our cultural creativity—secular and religious—largely was articulated in Judeo-Arabic and Arabic (Maimonides[1] being one of the few intellectuals to "make it" into the consciousness of the West); and even the most religious of our communities in the Middle East and North Africa never expressed themselves in Yiddish-accented Hebrew prayers, nor did they practice liturgical-gestural norms and sartorial codes favoring the dark colors of centuries-ago Poland. Middle Eastern and North African synagogues today—even in New York, Montreal, Paris, and London—have the winding quarter-tones of our music, which the uninitiated might imagine come from a mosque. North African and Middle Eastern Jewish women have never traditionally worn wigs[2]; hair covers, if worn, consisted of variations on regional clothing; in the wake of British and French imperialism, many women wore Western-style clothes.

Now that the three cultural topographies that compose my ruptured and dislocated history—Iraq, Israel, and the United States—have been involved in a war, it is crucial to say that Arab Jews exist. Some of us refuse to dissolve so as to facilitate neat national and ethnic divisions. My anxiety and pain, for example, during a Scud attack on Israel, where some of my family lives, did not cancel out my fear and anguish for the victims of the bombardment of Iraq, where I also have relatives.

But war is the friend of binarisms, leaving little place for complex identities. The Gulf War intensified a pressure already familiar to the Arab Jewish diaspora in the wake of the Israeli-Arab conflict: a pressure to choose between being a Jew and being an Arab. Since ancient times, our families have lived in the land that is today Iraq. Forty years ago, they were abruptly dislodged and moved to Israel. To be forced suddenly to assume a homogeneous European-Jewish identity based on experiences in Russia, Poland, and Germany was an exercise in self-devastation. To be a European or an American Jew hardly has been perceived as a contradiction, but to be an Arab Jew has been seen as a kind of logical paradox, even an ontological subversion. This binarism has led many Mizrahi/Sephardi Jews to a profound and visceral schizophrenia, since for the first time in our history Arab-ness and Jewish-ness have been imposed as antonyms.

Intellectual discourse in the West highlights a Judeo-Christian tradition, yet rarely acknowledges the Judeo-Muslim culture of the

Middle East, North Africa, pre-Expulsion Spain (pre–1492), or the European parts of the Ottoman Empire. The Jewish experience in the Muslim world often has been portrayed as an unending nightmare of oppression and humiliation. I in no way want to idealize that experience; there was tension, discrimination, and violence. On the whole, however, we lived quite comfortably within Muslim societies.

Generally, as Iraqi Jews, we were well-integrated and indigenous to the country, forming an inseparable part of its social and cultural life while retaining a communal identity. We used Judeo-Arabic in hymns and religious ceremonies. The liberal and secular trends of the twentieth century engendered an even stronger association of Iraqi Jews and Arab culture, which brought Jews into an extremely active role in public and cultural life. Prominent Jewish writers, poets, and scholars played a vital role in Arab culture, distinguishing themselves in Arabic-speaking theater, in music, as singers, composers, and players of traditional instruments. In Egypt, Morocco, Syria, Lebanon, Iraq, and Tunisia, Jews became members of legislatures, of municipal councils, of the judiciary, and even occupied high economic positions. The finance minister of Iraq in the 1940s, for example, was Ishak Sasson, and in Egypt, Jamas Sanua—higher positions, ironically, than those our community has generally achieved within the Jewish State.

Between 1948 and 1950, Middle Eastern and North African Jews were dispossessed of their property, lands, and roots in Muslim countries. As refugees or mass immigrants (depending on one's political perspective), we were forced to leave everything behind and give up our passports. This same process also affected our uprootedness and ambiguous positioning within Israel itself: We systematically were discriminated against by

Israeli institutions which deployed their energies and material resources to the consistent advantage of Ashkenazi Jews and to the consistent disadvantage of Mizrahi/Sephardi Jews.

Our physical features betrayed us, leading to internalized colonialism or physical misperception. Mizrahi/Sephardi women often bleached their dark hair blond, while the men more than once were arrested or beaten when mistaken for Palestinians. What for Ashkenazi immigrants from Russia and Poland was a social *aliyah* (literally "ascent") was for Mizrahi/Sephardi Jews a *yerida* ("descent").

Stripped of our history, we have been forced by our no-exit situation to repress our collective nostalgia, at least within the public sphere. The pervasive notion of "one people" reunited in their ancient homeland actively unauthorizes any affectionate memory of life before Israel. We have never been allowed to mourn a trauma that the images of Iraq's destruction only intensified and crystallized for some of us. Our cultural creativity in Judeo-Arabic, Arabic, Hebrew, and Aramaic is hardly studied in Israeli schools, and it is becoming difficult to convince our children that we actually did exist in, and that some of us still live in, Iraq, Morocco, and Yemen.

The notion of "in-gathering from exile" does not permit narration of the exile of Arab Jews in the Promised Land. My parents and grandparents, thirty or forty years after they left Baghdad, still long for its sights and sounds. Oriental Jews in Israel are enthusiastic consumers of Jordanian, Lebanese, and Egyptian television programs and films; just as our Oriental-Arabic music is consumed by the Arab world, often without its being labeled as originating in Israel. The Yemenite-Israeli singer Ofra Haza, for example, has been recognized by the Yemenites as continuing cultural tradition from Yemen.

Back in the days before the horrific bombing of Baghdad, my family and I used to play a bittersweet game of scanning the television to spot changes in the city's urban topography. But the impossibility of ever going back there once led me to contemplate an ironic inversion of the Biblical expression: "By the waters of Zion, we sat and wept, when we remembered Babylon."[3]

In the United States, watching media images of the Middle East gives one the impression that there are only European-American Jews in Israel and only Arab Muslims in the rest of the Middle East and North Africa. In the media, one finds few images of Palestinian-Israelis or of Iraqi-, Moroccan-, or Ethiopian-Israelis, even though non-Ashkenazim have comprised the majority of the Jewish population in Israel.

During the Gulf War, for example, most Israelis interviewed by American reporters tended to be European-Israelis, often speaking English with an American accent. This elision was especially striking when the missiles hit Ramat Gan—a city well known for its Iraqi population, popularly nicknamed "Ramat Baghdad." (A local joke had it that the Scuds fell there because they smelled the *amba*, an Iraqi mango pickle.)

It also stood out when the missiles hit poverty-stricken Iraqi-Jewish neighborhoods in the south of Tel Aviv: Television networks referred to these areas as "working-class neighborhoods," effacing their ethnic/racial/cultural identity as one would by calling Harlem a working-class neighborhood of New York City.

Some Iraqi Jews, furthermore, living in the United States, Britain, and Israel still have families in Iraq. The media showed images of prayers in the mosques and even the churches of Baghdad, but there was no reference to prayers in the synagogues there. In the American context, it is only the story of

European Jews that is narrated, denying Arab Jews the possibility of self-representation.

As an Iraqi Jew, I cannot but notice the American media's refusal to value Iraqi life. During the first Gulf War, the crippled animals in the Kuwait Zoo received more sympathetic attention than civilian victims in Iraq. The media much prefers the spectacle of the triumphant progress of Western technology to the survival of the peoples and cultures of North Africa and the Middle East. The case of Arab Jews is just one of many elisions. From the outside, there is little sense of our community, and even less sense of the diversity of our political perspectives. Mizrahi/Sephardi peace movements, from the Black Panthers of the 1970s to the more recent East for Peace and Oriental Front groups in Israel, Perspectives Judeo-Arabes in France, and the New York–based World Organization of Jews from Islamic Countries, not only call for a just peace for Israelis and Palestinians, but also for the cultural, political, and economic integration of Israel/Palestine into the Middle East and North Africa. They thus call, as do I, for an end to the binarisms of war, an end to a simplistic charting of Middle Eastern identities.

IN EXILE AT HOME

●

I *finish preparing the final segment of my radio interview*
with two women psychiatrists, regarding Ayatollah
Khomeini's death. I hand the tape over to the sound engi-
neer, get in my car, and head home.

    It is 4:00 P.M., Monday, June 5, 1989. Little less then forty-
eight hours have passed since Khomeini's death. The words I have
heard about him over the past two days run through my head in
an endless loop: bitter, vindictive, single-minded, powerful, insen-
sitive, murderous, religious, fanatic, unforgiving, ruthless.

    I am driving down Sunset Boulevard, deeply depressed. My
thoughts and work schedule have been so overloaded the last couple
of days that I have had no time to be alone, to think about what
has happened. Now that I have found some time, I am taken back
almost eleven years, and those same feelings—emptiness, sorrow,
and grief—again take over my entire being. I can barely see, as I
drive unfocused, guided by instinct, remembering that horrible
day, a day I have recalled time and again, but only speak of for
the first time.

It is October 6, 1978 (Mihr 14, 1357). As usual, I drop the kids off at school and head toward Ferdowsi Boulevard, towards my office at *Keyhan,* one of Iran's leading daily papers. Everyone is steadfastly at work in the newsroom. I head towards the telex room, to pick up the day's accumulated news from the France-Presse telex machine and begin translating it.

"France-Presse has no news today!" says the man in charge of the telex.

"How can there be no news?" I ask with astonishment. "France and Paris are the center of news for us Iranians now. Khomeini landed in Paris today; we must have gotten news of it!"

"No," he insists. "Nothing has arrived. I'll bring it to you when it gets here."

I return to my desk and busy myself reading foreign and national papers, waiting. I receive no news and leave the office at the end of my day, 1:00 P.M., heading home bewildered. I assume the news release must have been censured, but after complaining about it to myself for a few minutes, I put it out of my mind.

When the paper is delivered that afternoon, I read numerous reports from the French news headquarters on the first, second, and third pages, including news of Khomeini's arrival in Paris. I assume the news reports were wired after I left.

The next morning, I go to the telex room and, like the previous day, the man in charge claims to have no news from France-Presse. I return to my desk in News Services and sit there, not doing anything, while the other reporters run around, busily researching their articles. I watch them all out of the corner of my eye.

Their faces look slightly different—expectant, as if something is about to happen. People whisper into each other's ears. There is great commotion at the desks of *Keyhan*'s national section, predominantly occupied by leftist reporters. They communicate in an unusual sign language, making faces, speaking in gestures. I return to the telex room again and again: "No news has been wired!" I am told repeatedly.

"When did last night's reports come in?" I press.

"I don't know!" the attendant shrugs.

I go back to the newsroom and demand work from the editor of my department, Mr. N.A.—a middle-aged, companionable man who often enjoys a good drink or two, a friendly game of poker, and other complementary social vices. "Well here's a first," he laughs. "I've never heard anyone complain about not working. Until now, everyone complained about too much work! Go to the library and read a book. Find something to keep yourself busy."

"But Khomeini is in Paris now," I persist. "Paris is the center of news. France-Presse should be wiring reports by the ton!" And then I add jokingly, "It's not every day that French translators get to stand center stage, you know!" Mr. N.A. pays no attention to my joke, and sends me out of his office.

Day Three, 10:00 A.M.: The issue has become serious. The news reports are not reaching my desk, but their translations are being printed up every night. Though I see Mr. N.A. is working frantically on the day's paper, I walk into his office and interrupt him. "Would you mind telling me why someone else is translating my reports, while I am constantly being told that France-Presse isn't sending any news?"

"You're sticking your nose where it doesn't belong, little girl," Mr. N.A. replies. "Why don't you go back to your little desk and translate articles for other sections like Family Affairs, or write one of those inflammatory articles you're so famous for, and we'll talk later."

I am fed up with not working, with the secretive talk, and

with the incoherent stories everyone is telling me. I have never been good at dealing with people whispering, making insinuating gestures, and sharing secrets. I lose my temper. "First of all," I reply in a bitter tone, "I am not a little girl. I am a fully grown woman. Second, I am not sticking my nose where it doesn't belong. I am making direct inquiries about my personal business in this office. And third, I am not moving from your desk until I find out exactly what is going on."

Mr. N.A. looks at me with anger and hatred in his eyes, a look that quickly turns into one of belittling and humiliating contempt. He takes his reading glasses off the tip of his nose, "What are you thinking, little girl? You think they're gonna let some Jew translate reports on Ayatollah Khomeini? And a woman Jew at that? The news will get defiled."[1]

And so, on October 8, 1978, at 10:30 A.M., I am struck dumb, losing all sense of coherence in *Keyhan*'s newsroom where I have spent the last twelve years of my life working and writing. It is as if someone has just pulled the rug out from under my feet.

I return to my desk and collapse on my chair. Like a windup doll, I open my desk drawers and look inside: some scattered newspaper clippings, papers, writings, one dictionary, a few empty pen cases. I drop the key inside, close the drawer, pick up my bag, and leave, slowly walking down the hallway, as *Keyhan*'s newsroom spins around me.

By the time I reach the stairs, the tears have welled up in my eyes, blinding me to my own feet. I am so confused and bewildered that I have no idea what I am doing.

In the car, I come to the parking lot's iron gates and honk for Mr. Mehdi to let me out. Mr. Mehdi forces open the heavy gates. "Good day, Sister!"[2] he says, as I drive by him. I stare in astonishment; this is the first time Mr. Mehdi has called me "sister." He always has called people by their last names, along with the respective titles "Mr." or "Mrs."

On this autumn day, in the midst of the chaos on Ferdowsi Boulevard, I feel more alone and alienated than ever before in my life. I do not want to believe what I have just heard. Like a snake shedding its skin, Mr. N.A.—a man I have come to respect as an educated, intellectual, cultured, well-mannered, and insightful individual—has transformed in front of my very eyes.

While the sun still shines on the leaves and branches of the trees along Sunset, I remember the tears I shed that day behind the wheel on Ferdowsi. Those same feelings of emptiness, loneliness, and burdensome pain that wrenched my heart become real again. I get to the ocean, park the car, and look at the sunset, just as I watched it when I got home that fateful day—staring out the kitchen window toward the Alborz Mountains.

Long ago, I lost my self-consciousness about being a woman in a patriarchal society, and I have not thought about religion in years. In fact, I have argued time and again with my elders whenever they have recalled incidents of religious discrimination in rural towns. I have accused them of exaggerating, or I have claimed the world and its people have changed. And here I am, sitting in my house alone and disillusioned, desperately needing someone to tell me everything will be all right.

I call Farideh, an old friend. She is a journalist also, so we understand each other well. We regard ourselves as avant-garde, pioneering women of our society. As I fight back tears, I tell Farideh what has happened. She listens, and while trying to be as sensitive as possible, replies, "Look, sweetheart . . . Well . . . I mean, you're different from the rest of your people and all; you don't have any set prejudices, and you're not religious or anything like that. But if you ask me, I think you Jewish people should best return to your own country. You will all be better off there!"

I have no idea what she is talking about. "Our own country?" I ask. "Do we have a country besides Iran to call our own?"

"You know what I mean," she responds. "Why are you playing stupid? I am talking about Israel. You people already send all your money there, why don't you just go live there and spare yourselves the extra headache?"

This time I am not dumbstruck; rather, I am enraged, and I yell furiously: "If Israel is my country, then Arabia is yours! Why don't you try going back there, because you came to Iran 1,400 years after I did. When your people invaded Iran, we had already been living here for 1,400 years!" I scream and yell, and she screams and yells. I slam down the phone, get out of my seat, and frantically pace the room.

It is getting cold outside, and the cool and misty ocean breeze blows gently against my face. The fresh air slowly calms me down. I get back into the car, turn around, and head home, but not to the home where I shouted at Farideh, insulted by her and insulting her in return. Farideh. My one-time friend and colleague, who had been like a sister to me. It has been years since I have heard from Farideh, Mr. N.A., or countless others.

A neighbor from upstairs rushes down to my apartment in a panic, asking why I am shouting and crying. "Dear Farzaneh," I respond in tears, "Ayatollah Khomeini has opened Pandora's box. That old man has left us battered and defenseless. This exiled religious fanatic has unleashed a beastly ogre upon us, whose taming is all too impossible. Ayatollah Khomeini has destroyed all boundaries of respect between Muslims, Jews, Bahais, and Christians, turning brothers against each other."

"Don't upset yourself," Farzaneh says soothingly. "This is all temporary. Everything will go back to normal, nothing is going to happen." With that, she goes back upstairs, to her child who is calling.

Farzaneh's attempt to console me has been in vain. I am exiled in my own country, and I know it. An idea begins taking shape in my mind. I desperately try to shake it out of my head, to cast it away before it settles in my thoughts. But my attempts are futile. I lean my head against the hallway wall and say to myself, for the first time in my life, *We have to leave this place!*

On October 8, 1979, the ayatollah robbed me of my country. Since then, whenever I hear his name in relation to any event, an overwhelming pain of separation and isolation takes over my entire being, casting me into a state of lonesome emptiness. Ayatollah Khomeini's name, whether spoken or unspoken, reminds me of my separation: from my roots, from my home, from my work, from my friends. And in one instant, I see all of the people of Iran and notice how they have all shed their skins: Where soft and kind skin once was, poisonous thorns of enmity, discord, and hatred have now grown.

HOME IS WHERE YOU MAKE IT

I can honestly say that I never have procrastinated over a piece of writing as much as I have over this one. What is there to put off? Yet another opportunity to talk about identity, experience, history? I find that I am tired, not only of writing in the first person, but of reading experiences written in the first person. This is perhaps a particularly feminist state of literary exhaustion—so much feminist writing, particularly in anthologies, is about people exploring their identities on paper, sharing their struggles, heartaches, isolation, and journeys.

In the face of almost complete historical silence of the voices of women of color, it has been an essential literary and political strategy to write and publish these stories. Yet it seems that most of these personal narratives share a similar, almost evangelical pattern, hardly an original one, wherein the writer struggles toward a realization she proposed at the outset: and then I found a community. Amazing grace, once I was lost, but now I am found. Like many art forms that emerge out of oppositionality, there is a kind of aesthetic discomfort that accompanies these kinds of writings, as though they fail, in their plaintiveness and marginality, to succeed as art.

Perhaps this narrative form has become standard because so many discussions of identity are inherently focused on the search for home or community. But what happens when you make your home on the margins, that is, when you build your identity on instability—in what Audre Lorde calls "the very house of difference?" As Arab Jews in North America, we are marginally everything—marginally Jewish because we are not Ashkenazi, marginally Arab because we are Jewish, marginally "of color" because we have "something not quite Canadian" (or American) in our faces. We are immigrants, with a Mizrahi/Sephardi past that seems to have disappeared and homelands to which we cannot return. We can characterize this historical moment as being one of profound instability, as well as possibility.

If I were to be somewhat lazy and step into the footsteps of the quest narrative, where would I wish to end up? Like many children of immigrants, I have an imaginary homeland, a fictional Morocco reconstructed out of family anecdotes, accents, tastes, smells, familiar gestures, and books. As a homeless person of sorts, born into an immigrant family in Canada and now living in the United States, I think of myself as having many constituencies and a community of friends from these constituencies.

This sense of homelessness makes me reach out in search of others who are like me. Beyond feeling comforted knowing there are other actively feminist, non-Ashkenazi Jewish women in the world, I often feel validated that their words echo so much of what I have experienced.

It also is good to know that other non-Ashkenazi women have banged their heads against the wall known as the Jewish community, which we recognize as an Ashkenazi establishment. For a while in my twenties, I was starting to think I was crazy and alone, but I have discovered from rare articles and interviews that there are other "crazies" out there. It is exactly this feeling of recognition that convinces me of the need to keep relating our quest narratives, our personal stories. Even if we remain homeless after our tales are told, we at least can recognize each other and share the journey.

Mizrahim and Sephardim in the West are doubly a people in diaspora: both within the larger Jewish diaspora and now, in the postcolonial era, from our most recent cultural homes throughout North Africa and the Middle East. Without the walls of the *mellah* keeping us together as a community, we are scattered even more. In addition, we are now in countries where the racial and religious paradigms are very different from those of our original homelands—paradigms that colonizing and settler nations like the United States and Israel have both inherited and fostered, paradigms which our very existence upsets on many levels. That is to say, race in the West is arranged along paradigms of white and not-white, while the race paradigm in Israel has been forcibly organized along lines of Jew and Arab. The Mizrahi and Sephardi experiences do not fit easily into either of these stories.

I think that we suffer another literal kind of invisibility, one in which our features are not immediately recognizable as belonging to one ethnicity or the other. This is probably true for a lot of Arabs. As far as how other people see me, I know that I usually get a confused visceral reaction, "So, what are you exactly?" Sometimes I play games to see how long I can put off telling people my origin story: "So what kind of name is Kyla?"

"Well, my parents were hippies."

"So where are you from?"

"I'm Canadian." And on and on, just to irritate whomever I am talking to.

The truth is that invisibility can be kind of fun. It allows for a certain flexibility of identification, a kind of public playfulness about the way people see us. And it points, in the end, to the total fiction of race and ethnicity—the fantasy that who someone is can be pinned down to her origins, the signs displayed on her body, the place she comes from, the place she calls home. When we have a kind of flexibility about ourselves, we can make everybody nervous in their assumptions about who and what we are. If we really want to play it up, Moroccans are particularly flexible in this way, coming from the crossroads of Africa, Europe, and the Middle East, right at the mouth of the Gibraltar. We are, after all, Arabic, Jewish, African, Spanish, Mediterranean, and whatever else we have mixed in there, in my case a bit of English and Irish.

A woman I know once told me, "You have some color, but I wasn't sure quite what." I do not see myself as particularly dark. I do, however, think that color is not the only issue that defines the experience of racism. I think people are sometimes afraid to say that, fearing it will be seen as an attempt to claim the currently "fashionable" position of experiencing oppression, or as an attempt to deny the racism experienced because of skin color.

What exactly are we competing for? Discussions around racism need to address (and have increasingly done so) not only color, shade, and tone, but also physique, facial features, body movement, language, traditions, and culture. It is the various permutations and combinations of these and other characteristics that define us all as "other" and sometimes "other-other."

In these post–9/11 days of terrible anti-Arab sentiment, where not only Arabs but also Sikhs and other South Asian communities have come under attack, it is clear we need to move these discussions along quickly.

When I first came into contact with identity politics at the end of high school, it was like, *Pow!* Right in the kisser! Who am I? Where do I fit in? At the time, placing myself in the discourse of race was painful and problematic, because I identified as many things.

I have been labeled brown, olive, yellow, and white, at different times. In addition to telling me I do not seem "quite Canadian," people also have said there is something "not quite Jewish" about me. If the reactions I get from people do not fall along the lines of confusion, they may exhibit Orientalism: "You look so exotic," "I'll bet you smoke hash," and "have you seen *Casablanca*?"

A good friend of mine recently asked why I was looking outside of myself for the answer to who I am. As with all things, one has to return to the beginning . . .

My mother is a Moroccan Jew, born and raised in Casablanca, who came to Canada when she was eighteen. She had me a few years later. I believe strongly that the child of an immigrant learns the country with her immigrant parent. In many ways, although I was born and raised here, I see Canada as both my culture and a foreign country: I find processed cheese, white Christianity, and Hockey Night in Canada both wildly exotic and deeply familiar. I both "get it" and don't "get it"—double vision.

Indeed, "fitting in" was a long-standing and painful issue for my family, which up until my generation primarily was comprised of women—immigrant, working-class Moroccan Jews, predominantly single mothers of one form or another. It is not just Canadian behavioral codes that we have not quite been able to figure out, but the emotional codes, as well. For me, the languages of affection—toward children, for instance—are Arabic and French. These are the languages I always want to use with my partner as well.

And yet, there is a very Canadian side of me, one that I have only recently come to connect with: my father's side. Also immigrants, my father's family came from England and Ireland, my grandfather on an eight-year indentured work contract. On September 12, 2002, my father died of cancer, in my arms. His gift to me, through his death, was to reconnect me with his family—so totally different from me, and at the same time, so absolutely Canadian and familiar. They have taught me to look at the differences outside of me, and to find those same differences within. It is, after all, useless and self-destructive to resent Anglo-European culture when it is half of what I am.

My mother's family was afraid my mother would be thrown in jail for her Zionist activities—half the reason why my mother was brought to Canada. My only memories of her speaking about Israel, however, are when she was arguing in support of Palestinian self-determination. She taught me not to believe that Palestinians were inferior or crazy or more violent than Israelis. She taught me that in Morocco, Arabs were our neighbors and our friends, despite our religious differences.

Historically, I know there were prejudicial laws and hostility toward Jews in Morocco. We were *dhimmis,* outsiders, aliens. We lived in the *mellah,* and until probably the late nineteenth or early twentieth century, Moroccan Jews were made to pay *dhimmi* taxes for the right to stay in the country. At various times in history, Moroccan Jews were restricted in the clothing we could wear, the jobs we could hold, and the places we could live.

At the same time, we were an integral part of Moroccan culture, and according to my grandmother's friends, King Hassan V made his son promise to protect the Jews, which he did for most of World War II. That said, a little-known fact is that Moroccan Jews were shipped out of Morocco to the European death camps, during the Holocaust. In fact, my grandmother told me that by the time the Allies landed in North Africa in 1945, the Moroccan government was completely infiltrated by the Nazis, including the police, and that lists of Jews had already been made up for exportation and extermination. At one point, all of the Jews in Casablanca were asked to go to the main stadium with all of their gold in four days' time. Three days later, the Allies landed.

We were not untouched by the Holocaust. And of course, we have our own history of oppression in North Africa, Spain, and the Middle East, as well as our own history of cultural production, survival, and creativity.

I did not grow up in much contact with the Jewish community, and I rarely dated or even socialized with North American Ashkenazi Jews. My trip to Israel as a teenager, and a lot of reflection on my experiences, have taught me that although we are Jews, Ashkenazim do not always accept Mizrahim and Sephardim as equal partners in Jewish life. In Israel, I heard Mizrahim and Sephardim referred to as *barbarim* (barbarians), and it is very clear to me that Mizrahim and Sephardim occupy a secondary place to Ashkenazim in Israel, despite the fact that we have been the majority Jewish population for decades. Along these lines, many Mizrahi and Sephardi Israeli women, including some in my own family, marry Ashkenazi men—particularly, religious Ashkenazi men. These women are seen as marrying up.

In North America as well, Ashkenazim have much more economic leverage than we do, as well as a longer history here and something of a place (albeit a problematic one) at the cultural table. As a result, if I tell people I am Jewish, they assume I am Ashkenazi. If I tell them I am Moroccan, they assume I am Muslim. And if I say I am a Moroccan Jew, they ask which of my parents is Jewish and which is Moroccan.

Claiming an African identity, particularly in a North American framework, is problematic, as people seem to forget that Morocco is a country in Africa. When I joined the African Students Group at my undergraduate university, for example, members looked skeptical. It was the Arab student group that welcomed me with open arms.

I had the same experience the first time I went to Morocco: As I passed through customs, the agent squinted at my passport, which says "Tompkins," the name I inherited from my father. The agent then looked up at me, confused. "Tompkins?" he said, *"Mais vous êtes d'origine Marocaine?"*

"Oui," I responded, *"Ma mère est Marocaine."*

"Ah. Bienvenue chez vous." ("Tompkins? But you're of Moroccan origin?" "Yes, my mother is Moroccan." "Ah. Welcome to your home.")

I strongly feel the need to preserve my Moroccan Jewish culture. When my great-grandmother died eight years ago, and then my grandfather only a few months ago, I felt not only the grief related to losing them, but a sense of mourning that Mizrahim and Sephardim are losing touch with their histories. Our entire culture is dying out, and I want to somehow fight this cultural death. I meant to record some anecdotal history with my great-grandmother, after whom I am named, but I never did, to my eternal grief. She lived through two world wars, British colonialism, French colonialism, Moroccan independence, and then at the age of sixty, immigration to Canada. Once she got to Toronto, she hardly ever left her apartment again, except on the High Holy Days.

What to do with this family history? My first concern is to preserve my heritage. It has become important to me not only to learn to speak Arabic, but to study and understand my people's history as well. At the same time, I am ambivalent about the ways in which Jews seem to separate themselves so much from the rest of the world, although I understand the historical reasons. In addition, the ways in which middle-class Jewish-ness has come to align itself so closely with whiteness is disturbing. The dominant Jewish identity of the last century or so has been built on the exclusion of people of color—North African, Arab, and sub-Saharan African. And yet, I love my Jewish people very much, which makes this struggle all the more painful.

In a sense, many of us are Jews without a Jewish community. The 1995 International Gay and Lesbian Jewish Conference in New York was an amazing example of this reality. The conference was held at a swanky hotel; the meals were expensive; and not one of the workshops looked at the issues of non-Ashkenazi Jews. Most of the workshops focused on religious issues and veered away from political ones such as gender, race, and class.

On the last day of the conference, I met one Moroccan Jewish man, and we both laughed about how the most Moroccan thing about the conference was the couscous they served on Saturday night—which any Moroccan Jew will tell you is exactly what you will never eat in a Moroccan house after *Shabbat* is over. It is too much work!

Perhaps when progressive Mizrahi and Sephardi Jews come together to talk, we will start to deal with the mainstream Jewish community together. My cousins and I talk about trying to build a progressive Sephardi congregation when we are all living in the same place. Until then, why bother taking up these battles? For me there are too many fronts on which to fight, and Ashkenazi institutions have proven only too often that they are not allies.

Last summer, I heard Judith Butler speak at a seminar at Cornell University. One of the things she said was that after 9/11, there is an ethical imperative to ask the question, "Who are you?" to each citizen of the world, and to always consider that question an open and unanswered one: one which has a beginning but no ultimate ending. Because as soon as we think we have found a singular answer for "the other" facing us, we already have reduced her or him.

The same must be true for our own search for self. I have long stopped looking for home. Home, I have learned, is where we sit down and decide to build it. And of course, this is the most profound lesson of the Diaspora, one that must necessarily change the shape of the identity narrative. Because if we leave open the question of where and what a home is, if we let it remain a question that has to be asked again and again and is never entirely answered, we accept that none of us have only one origin, whether ethnic, geographic, or religious. What we have is a more complicated narrative that intersects and intertwines with other citizens of the world, and remains, ultimately, forever unanswerable and open.

THE SEARCH TO BELONG

I have been a hybrid all my life, forever caught between two or more worlds. On good days, I find this multiculturalism unique and enriching. On bad days, it feels like a lifelong burden, an experience marked by alienation and schizophrenia. For starters, since Tunisia became a French protectorate in 1882 (what I have come to call an "historical accident"), I was born French to French parents who spoke nothing but French to me; yet, we were all Tunisian.

When I was three months old, my parents, sister, and I emigrated from Tunis to Nice, in the south of France. There I received an education steeped in the history of Charlemagne, *le bon roi* Saint Louis, and a whole gallery of Catholic queens, kings, nobility, church people, academics, and philosophers. I proudly sang the "Marseillaise" and could identify major cities on the map of France, but I had no idea of the shape of Tunisia or where it was, exactly. I grew up assimilated in an assimilated family, an atheist ignorant of Judaism except for our annual Pesah celebration at my paternal grandparents'. I was not sure how Moses fit into the picture; I never stepped into a synagogue as a child; and I did not return to Tunisia until I was thirty-five years old for a one-week visit.

My Tunisian roots nonetheless have formed my entire life. Since I was old enough to be conscious of my memories and mental images, the African continent has stirred me. Before I could say one intelligible word, I had visions of palm trees and the beating sun. Over the years, my attraction to my elusive native land turned into my own personal mythology.

I wish I spoke Arabic and the Judeo-Arabic dialect that filled my grandmother's speech with guttural sounds and priceless images: "The robber comes back with a lit candle," she would say of someone with a lot of nerve. *"Alawoucheck!"* (On your face!) she would mutter upon seeing a man spit in public.

I wish I had spent lazy summers on the white sandy beaches lined with dunes, beaches my mother described to me countless times. I wish I had heard the bell of the ice-cream man and the other street vendors roaming around Tunis after the *siesta,* selling roasted pistachios, pralines, slices of cold watermelon, and *granite*—lemon ice—in paper cornets. I wish historical circumstances had not torn me from my native land, where my ancestors had lived for generations, before I had a chance to savor it firsthand.

Surrounded by Tunisian Jews of my parents' generation, I grew up with other people's memories. Most of these people were childhood friends of my father's—often men who had played on the national volleyball team my father had captained in his late teens. Some still went by the nicknames they had gotten in their Boy Scout years, and the fact that grown men could be called *Canard* (Duck) or *Zèbre* (Zebra) with a straight face was enough to tickle me.

Though I rarely related to any of them directly, I watched these men intently. They added spice, laughter, and boundless animation wherever they went. They joked, teased each other, and bantered endlessly. They were fun and had fun, cut each other off constantly, accompanied each sentence with wide hand gestures, gave each other high-fives several times in the course of a conversation, and peppered their exchange with bits and pieces of Judeo-Arabic. I loved it when some of them—usually Sam and Minouche, who are single—hung out at our house, filling it with their sing-song North African accent and booming voices (soft-spoken Tunisian Jews are a rare species) and playing bridge with my parents. Minouche, a short stocky man with a thin mustache and glasses, was notorious for losing his temper while playing cards. My sister and I giggled in the dark at night, as soon as his familiar yells of outrage reached us from the living room on the floor below.

This Tunisian Jewish network gave me a warm sense of community and camaraderie I did not know for myself, growing up with my only sister in an isolated villa overlooking the spectacular Baie des Anges.

Aside from my father's friends, I learned about Tunisian Jewish culture from the food we ate. Even I, who then saw eating as more a chore than a pleasure, could not resist the spicy green and black olives and assorted nuts served as appetizers, or the array of small salads, the *kemia,* that preceded any traditional meal—artichoke hearts in lemon dressing, boiled carrots in cumin and garlic sauce, *slata mechouia* made with charbroiled peppers and tomatoes, crushed garlic, and fresh lemon juice.

My maternal grandmother prepared feasts that filled her apartment with distinctive, mouth-watering aromas. She always served couscous with all the trimmings—meatballs, potatoes, turnips, carrots, and chickpeas simmered in bouillon and infused with cumin and *harissa* (North African hot sauce). For dessert, she often made flour *yoyos* dipped in homemade, orange-scented honey. Her delicious quince preserves and apricot pie I have never tasted anywhere else. Everything was always fresh and made from scratch.

I grew up around women who showed their caring by feeding others. And so, as it was for my mother and my grandmothers, cooking has long been one of my favorite ways of giving.

In the 1960s, Tunisians comprised a large part of the North African immigrant community in southern France, and they were the only Jews we socialized with. I cannot recall contact with other Sephardim or Mizrahim (such as Moroccans or Algerians), and my uncle Marcel, then married to my father's sister, was the only Ashkenazi I knew. I grew up hearing jokes about the *yekes*, German Jews like him—about their fussiness, lack of humor, and above all, odd culinary customs. Once, my mother mistook Marcel's preparation of herring in cream sauce for dirty dish water, and she dumped the just-used plates, knives, and forks in it. The incident became legendary on our side of the family, and years later, we still roared with laughter at the memory. I was proud of being a Tunisian Jew and never failed to be entertained by the jokes and stories, the high sense of drama and verbal expressiveness of my community.

Growing up in Nice, I came into daily contact with native French Catholics, and as a child, I had very positive bonds with some of them—first with Mémé Paul, the old woman who worked as our nanny from the time I was about three. She taught my sister and me French folk songs, while taking us on long walks around country roads. I loved her and her twenty-year-old grandson Alain, a tall, lean, dark-haired man. His forever smiling eyes, patience, genuine kindness, and charming accent—so typical of the southeast of France—made him an ideal man in my eyes. (I proposed to him when I was six and was temporarily crushed when he married a woman his own age.)

Alain was born out of wedlock, and he and his family were village people—unprejudiced, open, and generous. Ethnic origins and religion were never mentioned and simply were not issues to them. Neither were they issues with our old neighbors, Monsieur and Madame Lafeuillade, who owned the property adjacent to the villa we rented on the Mont Boron, with the Nardins who lived across the street, or with my elementary school friend Martine. I was able to live in two different worlds and draw a sense of delight and identity from both.

My self-image changed drastically as soon as I entered the Lycée Calmette. I remember standing in line in the schoolyard with my new classmates on the first day of school when they called out my name. The name I had never questioned before turned into a source of ridicule and ostracism at that moment. It singled me out of the vast majority of Catholic girls and turned me into the butt of jokes. "Smadja" was so obviously foreign, so "un-French."

From that day on, I learned to feel ashamed of the heritage I proudly had taken for granted. I came to believe that being a "true French" was the highest standard, if not the only acceptable one, and that I was a fake everyone could see through. The coolest girls in the class quickly renamed me "Maharaja," and so my name, the name of my ancestors, became a source of dread and self-loathing.

It was not long before the sneers focused on my physical

traits. The first time I dared wear lipstick in public, some of my classmates hissed "nigger lips" at me in the schoolyard. I was not yet thirteen. It was only years later, miles and oceans away, that I stopped thinking of my mouth as a curse and began seeing it as an asset, savoring the irony of Hollywood actresses resorting to collagen implants to create a sensual pout.

I must have been in eighth grade when one of the "untouchables" in our class took me aside at recess one day and, to my bewilderment, asked me to follow her into a deserted classroom. She then asked me point-blank, with the enigmatic airs of a CIA agent, "Are you Israelite?" I only had heard the word *juive* up to then. "If anybody asks, say you're Jewish," my mother had admonished me. I recognized the name "Israel" and could tell my classmate was steering me in a dangerous direction. I felt shame at not clearly understanding the label, and even more shame that I was someone who would *fit* this label.

I looked blankly at this girl for a moment, not daring to ask what she meant. Finally I answered, as if apologizing, *"Je suis juive* (I am a Jew)." Her turquoise-penciled eyes lit up with triumph as she burst out, "I knew it! I *knew* you were Israelite!" She rushed out of the room without another look, leaving me alone with my back to the blackboard, feeling that "Jewish" must be a dirty word, since she had not let it escape her rouged lips.

This incident illuminates the trouble I faced during the four interminable years I stayed at the Lycée Calmette. Being ostracized for being different was bad enough. Worse was not really knowing why or how I was different, being a Jew with no clear connections to Judaism. I had been taught nothing of my religion or history. On Yom Kippur, I went to school and ate. I had never heard of Rosh Hashanah nor read a line from the Old

Testament. Had I been training for my bat mitzvah, I would have had something of my own to fall back on, when students pressed me with the question, "Why aren't you preparing your second communion like the rest of us?" I had no spiritual beliefs to hold onto.

This reality, probably as much as the taunting, led to a fragmented identity that sealed my sense of self as "the other"—someone permanently divided, someone alienated from her own roots, culture, and language. I still cannot bring myself to check identity boxes when filling out forms. The word "Jewish" is nowhere to be found, and the word "Caucasian" sounds weird and removed from me. I leave them blank every time, with the renewed feeling that what and who I am does not fit into any category.

Truth is, I have been an expatriate since I was three months old; I just did not fully realize it until my thirties. My mother tells me that when we all left Tunis for Nice, I was so small she carried me in a basket "like little Moses." My sister remembers that I cried every night for six months after our arrival on the French Riviera. I do not remember any of it directly, but the pain of what turned out to be my second experience with involuntary exile is still as vivid as a stab.

I was fourteen when my parents, shaken by the Six-Day War of a few years earlier, decided we would make *aliyah* to Israel. Prior to our departure, my sister and I were submitted to a two-year crash course in being Jews. Our mother signed us up for the Dror, a Zionist youth organization. Overnight, we found ourselves learning Israeli folk songs and dances, hearing lectures about Theodore Hertzl, and watching newsreels of concentration camps. The pictures were so horrid and new to me that they felt unreal.

Typical for a bookworm like myself, it was only while reading *Exodus* that I had my first in-your-face moment. I realized that the mass genocide that had ended less than forty years earlier related to me personally, and that I, by an accident of birth and very much against my will, belonged to the Jewish people. The sheer terror of what had happened to my people—the betrayal, degradation, torture, unthinkable cruelty—made me sob uncontrollably.

As a fair-haired, light-eyed Jew, I was immediately cast as alien by my new Israeli neighbors, who were Mizrahi and Sephardi. As a middle-class Jew with a French education, I in turn was initially repulsed by them. As time passed, however, I came to realize that their destitution, illiteracy, and seeming lack of manners fit into a broader picture of unfair and demeaning treatment by mainstream Israeli society. My fear turned into sympathy.

As soon as I learned enough Hebrew to get a sense of what was being said, I was shocked at how much self-loathing there was among the young slum-dwellers of Katamon Tet—the same self-loathing that I since have felt coming from poor Black Americans, young men in particular. Once, my sister and I were walking with a few of the boys from the housing projects across the street, when one of them began to engage me in conversation.

"Where are you from?" he asked.

"*Ani mi Tzarfat* (I am from France)," I replied.

"Real France or, you know, the *other* France?" he sneered. By then, I was familiar with the "joke," sad rather than funny: Israelis from Morocco often claimed they were from France, so as to hide their true origins.

"I am French," I replied, nonplussed. "But I was born in Tunisia." We exchanged a few more words, and then he dropped with a self-deprecating laugh, *"Ani Moroco Sakin*—("I am a Moroccan knife)"—a term I had already heard around the neighborhood, used by dark-skinned, black-haired boys like him to refer to themselves and each other.

"How can you say this about yourself?" I shot back. "I'm proud to be a Sephardi. You should be too. There's nothing wrong with being from Morocco." With these words came the realization that as unlikely as it seemed, we were on the same side of the fence.

By a sad irony, it was in Israel that I was made fully aware of the split between Jews—Sephardim (a term which at the time also meant Mizrahim) and Ashkenazim—and of the fact, perplexing to me then and now, that the latter felt superior to us. In Israel, as in the Lycée Calmette, I found myself part of a despised minority. In Nice, I had been a not-quite-good-enough French, and in Israel, I was a not-quite-good-enough Jew. The difference was that this time, I reacted with anger, not shame.

Although both my coloring and social class shielded me from direct prejudice, I resented mainstream Israeli society for giving Sephardim an inferior status and a bad reputation. While school programs emphasized the works and achievements of Cholom Halehem, I thought of the greatness of Maimonides, a chief contributor to the Spanish Golden Age and one of the most brilliant Jewish intellectuals of all times.

Less than twenty years after the birth of the modern Jewish state, the vast majority of Jews from North Africa and the Middle East lived at the bottom of the socioeconomic ladder. They were predominantly poor, uneducated people who worked as maids, garbage collectors, and manual laborers, conspicuously absent from the political power structure and liberal professions. To this day, Mizrahim are portrayed as right-wing extremists who are ruining the peace process, too dumb to realize they are being manipulated by demagogues. Sadly, this image, prevalent in Israel, is being reinforced by the American press.

Because of my looks and because I was seen as French, not as Sephardi, I did not suffer personally from this hostile environment. In fact, my experience as a ninth-grader enrolled in an Israeli high school ended up being the most positive school year of my life. Beit Sefer Denmark was a new, progressive school; its egalitarian philosophy required that all students wear the same uniform to downplay socioeconomic disparities. Never in my life have I attended a more diverse learning institution. Sephardim, Mizrahim, Ashkenazim, and a few non-Jews all studied together.

Jerusalem in the early seventies was the most nonurban city I have ever visited. Though a paved road led to Denmark, as we called our school, one had to walk on stretches of sand before getting there. The only sign of human life on the way was a *makolet*—a tiny, decrepit grocery store found in the most incongruous of places, selling everything from soap to canned food.

Starting a new year in a brand new country where I did not want to live, and being schooled in a new language I had far from mastered, were at first bewildering, if not excruciating, experiences. English became my first language in a matter of days. My adaptation took a painful six months, during which I fended off all rapprochement by my Israeli classmates while keeping in check the ardor of the American boys. And yet, going from an oppressive all-girls school to a mixed one where students came in all colors, cultures, and backgrounds was nothing short of a personal liberation.

Books became my main connection to French culture, and being severed from my native tongue and the country that had been mine turned me into an even more voracious reader than before. This passion for literature drew me out of my silence. The first time I spoke up in class, speaking in Hebrew, was to make a comment about *L'Avare* by Molière. Our literature teacher nearly keeled over in shock, as I had spent a full six months not saying a word, drawing portraits of imaginary people on the blank pages of my notebook.

The fact that I could draw won me endless praise and attention from my Israeli classmates. Girls rushed over to me at recess to ask for their portraits, and I was put in charge of decorating the class for Purim. My popularity was so new and unexpected that it floored me most of the time. I did not know how to respond to compliments, and I felt embarrassed when crumpled love notes landed on my desk. But I did savor the company, support, and sympathy of boys and girls my age and the unique, wonderful feeling of being part of a group—of being wanted, of belonging.

I would have loved nothing more than to remain in that environment, but things were falling apart on the home front. After a year in Israel, my family had moved into our own apartment in the brand new neighborhood of Ramat Eshkol. My father had resigned from his job, and month after month he lounged in the living room in near-total lethargy. My mother spent a lot of time in her painting studio, and she complained daily to my sister and me about my father and their crumbling marriage. The situation could not last.

I sensed I needed to resume my French studies to prepare for the *Baccalauréat,* the dreaded exam that awaits all French students at the end of high school, so I transferred to the Lycée Français. My social life dropped to a near-zero in a matter of weeks. There were only four boys in the entire school, and most students came from highly dysfunctional families. Some kids had drug problems, and a number of girls slept around at the risk of getting pregnant. After the multicultural, yet cohesive, wholesome environment of Denmark, the lycée felt like stepping into a psycho ward. I went back to my loner ways, dove into my studies, and began to prepare for the *Bac* with a determination I, let alone the rest of the family, did not know I had.

I had made the right decision. Two months after the end of the school year, my parents declared their *aliyah* a failure, and the family returned to France. We left our furnished apartment in the care of a friend, with most of our lifelong possessions still in it. We "kids"—I was sixteen, my sister nearly eighteen—were not asked about our preference, and once again, we were uprooted against our will. By that time, I had come to love Israel—its sparseness, the vulnerability behind the fierce at-war mask, the genuineness and no-nonsense approach of native Israelis, the warmth, generosity, and reliability I found behind their bluntness.

I had my first boyfriend in Israel, and I became more mature, wiser, and capable than I ever imagined possible. I felt like a sabra, protective and proud of my new country. I begged my mother to let me stay behind and go to boarding school, but she refused with a peremptory "A girl your age needs her family." In hindsight, I am glad she refused. I do not think I would have survived emotionally, alone in the disruptive ambiance of the Lycée Français.

Whereas my father went back to Nice in the hopes of salvaging his faltering business, my mother chose to settle in Paris, wanting to try out the excitement of the capital, and it was decided my sister and I would go with her.

My subsequent life there can be summed up as almost a decade of alienation. After fourteen years in provincial, laid-back Nice and two years in barely developed Jerusalem, the fast pace and high stress of Paris felt like a personal assault, to say nothing of the implacably gray sky hanging over the city like a menace. Growing up in Nice, I had heard constant jokes about Parisian snobbery, arrogance, and stressful lifestyle. True to their reputation, most Parisians turned out to be sectarian, unwelcoming, and aggressive.

Through well-connected friends of my parents, I was enrolled at Victor Duruy, my fourth high school in three years, one which catered to the chi-chi crowd. One of the only friends I made that year was a French-American girl, an Ashkenazi Jew who also felt out of place among the Parisian-born upper crust.

To add to my isolation and grief over leaving Israel, the Yom Kippur War exploded less than two months after our move. It shocked me deeply, boosted my newfound Zionism, and heightened my sense of being brutally cut off from my recent past and roots. But there was no one to turn to with my feelings. My mother was busy starting a new life as a single woman with two teenage daughters, and since the onslaught of puberty, my sister and I had stopped confiding in each other.

I felt ill at ease in Paris, in exile in my own country. From the first day there, I dreamed of my escape. Pragmatism led me to first focus on the *Bac,* which I passed on the first try. Next, since I had a knack for languages, I decided to enroll as an English as a Second-Language major at the University in the Marais. I missed my interaction with English speakers, as well as the language itself. I made many connections there among my peers, spent countless hours with them rebuilding the world over a cup of coffee, and enjoyed some of the most stimulating conversations of my life. But I built no lasting bonds and made no close friends.

I shared with people little or nothing of my experience in Jerusalem, as I found no one who could relate. In fact, I felt conflicted about, if not outright ashamed of, my Zionism. In the Parisian university circles of the mid to late '70s, being anti-Zionist was de rigueur, fashionable. At the all-leftist, pro-Palestinian film department of Censier, one of my sister's classmates declared to our face that most of the world's problems were due to the wealthy *juiverie internationale* (international Jewry). My sister stayed mute, but I considered it my duty to put this guy back in his place. He apologized to us in response.

Paris has a significant Mizrahi/Sephardi population, clustered in several neighborhoods, including rue Montmartre close to the Folies Bergère, but my family had no roots there. My life as the daughter of failed middle-class people (my father's business had ended in bankruptcy) was circumscribed by where I lived and studied. In addition, my perception of Paris was entirely colored by the fact that I did not want to be there and that I felt like an alien as long as I stayed. Leaving became an obsession, my ticket to the future.

Going back to Israel was my natural choice. Having had a taste of kibbutz life but never more than two weeks at a time, I signed up as a volunteer at Givat Brenner, one of the largest kibbutzim in the country. I worked in the aluminum factory, picked grapes and citrus in the orchards, and met young people from Scandinavia, Germany, Australia, England, and the United States.

My experiences were all enriching experiences I could not have had anywhere else. As a volunteer, however, I was cut off from the Israelis, the kibbutzniks. Kibbutz life, which is inherently autarchic, also cut me off from mainstream Israeli society and culture. Bored, directionless, and missing my family, I returned to Paris after six months and resumed my studies. When I became a major in American Civilization, my attraction to American people and culture, born several years earlier in Jerusalem, turned to outright fascination. Feeling no more at home in Paris than before my trip to Israel, it became clear that my next destination must be the United States, that my destiny, the new life that awaited me, was inextricably linked to the New World.

I am grateful to America for giving me the freedom and opportunity to become my own person, for giving me a sense of home I thought was unattainable. Even after more than twenty years, though, I am still an alien in many ways. Ironically, I feel most estranged in the community that is supposed to be mine.

I have a number of Ashkenazi friends who are welcoming and unprejudiced, but as a group, American Jews have an ethnocentric view that ignores the very existence of people like me. They assume all Jews originate from Eastern Europe; they think of Yiddish as the only Jewish language besides Hebrew; and they presume that all worthwhile Jewish leaders, artists, and thinkers are Ashkenazi.

Every time I have tried to take part in American Jewish communities, I have been faced, once again, with the feeling of being different, not fitting in. Lost among people who delight in matzo ball soup and can barely locate Tunisia on a world map, I have yet to find a place where I can be myself without feeling invisible, dismissed, or treated like a rare, exotic species. As a result, I am still haunted by the need to belong.

My attraction to the African continent is heightening day by day, and I find it seeping through my fiction writing. Without my planning it, my stories unfold in the maze of Fez, along the coast of Cameroon, through the *souks* of Tunis, and among the remote villages of the Sudan. More than ever, it is both my Jewish identity and my African heart that guide my life, real and imagined, as I continue the search for a community to call my own.

HENRIETTE DAHAN KALEV

ILLUSION IN ASSIMILATION

"Y ou are so pretty; you don't look Moroccan."

I grew up with this sentence, since the day my parents brought me from Morocco to Israel in 1949. I heard it from the nurse, dressed in white, who spoke of raising children as though it were a Zionist invention. She came to the immigrant camp to advise my mother on how to raise me, my sister, and my baby brother, who was born in our tent.

I heard it from my tall, silver-haired German Jewish kindergarten teacher. She took my name, Henriette, from me, and in its place, she gave me the awful name Ahuva. "'Henriette,'" she said, "is too hard to pronounce, both for me and the other children."

I heard it from the neighbors. I heard it throughout my adolescence when, upon first meetings, special attention was given to my looks. Today as an adult, when wrinkles have begun to carve my face, the sentence has been refined to "Really? You don't look it."

My so-called non-Moroccan look enabled me more than once to turn into something like *Sesame Street*'s Snuffleupagus, who could see but was not seen. I frequently heard opinions about Moroccans from the mouths of non-Moroccans who took me for one of their own. As such, I learned a great deal about inclusion and exclusion, superiority and inferiority in Israeli society of the 1950s and 1960s.

Early on, at age four, the aforementioned sentence already provoked in me vague feelings somehow related to the tension between my relatively light complexion and my origin. Only later did I understand these feelings as the subtext of "I am *lucky* I don't look Moroccan."

At a young age, I also grasped the notion of inherent conflict between aesthetic value and anything Moroccan. This notion was first exemplified when my mother complained about my class-mates' hostility toward me. My teacher did not bother relating to the content of my mother's complaint. Instead, she said my mother was behaving like a pushy street peddler and that "there [was] no room for such vulgarity and primitivity in our school."

My father had transferred me to this "better" school in Holon, named after a great Zionist thinker, Moshe Helss, as part of an effort to have his children assimilate quickly and effi-ciently. A "better" school meant one attended by children of veteran immigrants—pioneers, preferably Ashkenazi.

All of the children were indeed Ashkenazi. They also hap-pened to be the children of artists and politicians, and they all participated in extracurricular enrichment programs such as ballet, piano, and violin. For a while, I too attended an enrich-ment program, taking a painting class out in the sand dunes of Holon. I loved to paint and apparently showed some talent, but my father, who was worried about my formal education, soon let me know I would be "better off reading a book than wasting time out in the dunes."

My sense of alienation during my childhood turned upon this axis: I did not look Moroccan, and so I was "lucky." I *did* look Ashkenazi, and so I was "very lucky." Trapped between who I was and who people thought I was, my world view crystallized according to a clear dichotomy of good and bad, based on origin.

When I was ten, my father was promoted at work, and my parents moved to Jerusalem. This move gave me the opportunity to open a new page in my life: Since no one knew me, I could invent a new self-image and escape from being one of the "ugly Moroccans." I told new friends that I was born in France. From that time on, I spent my time constructing and protecting the child I wanted to be—the French child. To be convincing, I eliminated my distinctive Arabic accent when pronouncing the letters *het* and *'ayin*, and I trained myself to adopt the typical Ashkenazi pronunciations, *chet* and *ayin*. I never invited any of my friends home, so as not to risk having them discover my real life. I even forbade my mother from speaking Arabic in the street.

Soon, even I began to believe my own deceptive tales, and little by little I constructed a desirable identity for myself. I asked my parents about French words, since they had studied at the Alliance Israelite French colonial school in Morocco. I asked them about French history and culture, and long before the general history classes began in school, my mother had taught me about Zola, Hugo, *Les Miserables*, Rousseau and the Revolution, Napoleon and his battles, and General Lyotee.

I incorporated all this information into the identity I was weaving, and I added biographic details meant to ensure my acceptance in class. For example, I claimed that I studied fine arts—which was easy, since everyone studied fine arts. Later, I added that I studied dance. Everyone believed this claim, as well, since I had good physical coordination and loved athletics. Once, during a youth training course, I was asked to perform a dance piece. I made something up, which later I found out was called "improvisation," and it went over great.

As the two realities of home and school grew more and more distant from each other, I developed my tales and cushioned my world with soft, fluffy, and happy imaginative thoughts. I outdid myself when I bragged to my teacher in vocational high school that I had been chosen to participate in the Habima Youth. Habima is the Israeli National Theater Company. Habima Youth was an imaginary, nonexistent organization, which I said was meant to promote talented young actors. The teacher believed me and permitted me to leave class early every Tuesday.

It is clear now that the common denominator of all my tales, whether I was conscious of it or not, was Ashkenazi culture. I hated the real me. Me, the Moroccan, the non-French, the immigrant who didn't participate in enrichment programs like the other kids, who did no more than her very annoying school work.

I had to read and memorize entire books on the Jewish people throughout the "world," meaning throughout Eastern Europe. I had to read about my supposed ancestors in the *shtetl*, about the "family of fighters" who broke through to besieged Jerusalem, all of whom were European; and about the *Choma u Migdal,* the wall and tower of the pioneer kibbutzim, founded by European Jews. I never found the real me in these books.

In despair, I stopped studying, and I became more certain that I should hold onto that imaginative French girl. *Mikraot Yisrael* (Roots of Israel) and *Historia shel Am Yisrael* (The

History of Israel), obligatory elementary school texts on Israeli history and literature, provided background for my invented European girl, and they reinforced my belief that the other girl, the real me, did not deserve to exist.

When I finally found texts written about the real me, I discovered that I was Mizrahi, described as dirty, poor, contagious with infectious diseases, spiritually impotent, lacking moral capacities, ignorant, violent, and lazy.[1] At best, my parents and I were described as "having fallen into an historical coma."[2] At worst, we were accused of bringing about the cultural demise of the *yishuv*—the Jewish Settlement—due to our inferiority complex as tribes and *edot*. *Edot* is the term used to describe something just short of "ethnicities," lest it be known that Jews do not constitute a singular "ethnic" group.[3] For Ashkenazim, "Jewish unity" seems predicated on a notion of sameness. The idea of Jews being a multiracial, multiethnic people somehow threatens Ashkenazi leadership.

After reading about the despicable qualities of Mizrahim, I had enough convincing evidence to justify the extermination of my hated Moroccan self. Even history said she was bad, and who wanted to be primitive and dirty?

I worked hard to acquire Ashkenazi knowledge and invested all my energy in it. I did it, however, as a thief in the night. I looked out of the corner of my eye to see what the other kids ate, how they played, and what they wore. I listened to their conversations about cello lessons, messy rooms, and the punishments their mothers gave. I visited their homes and checked to see how their rooms were furnished. I saw their little radios and observed them listening to *Hamasach Oleh*, "high" culture theatrical broadcast. I aspired to be like them, speak like them, be accepted by them.

Nothing that was mine (the real me) seemed appropriate to share in exchange; so I concentrated on refining my Ashkenazi costume, imitating the look and form. While my "friends" were succeeding in acquiring the "real thing," an in-depth study of the formal curriculum, I was failing. The teacher told my mother, "She could succeed and achieve if only she wanted to," and my mother made sure to repeat it to me. I truly wanted to succeed, but there was a limit to my capacity to absorb not only the canon, but the entire context in which that canon was rooted.

I was held back a grade and then sent to a vocational school to become a good cook. Later, I was expelled. Even in army courses, I could not make it. I was a failure in my teachers' eyes and my own. I was left imprisoned in an inner world, built on shattered bits and pieces of identities: a reflection of an Israeli, a despised Moroccan, and an imaginary French girl. My inner world was like a room full of mirrors.

A few years ago, I found myself leafing through a children's book, *Rumiah, the Little Nanny*.[4] The author, Levin Kipnis, received the Israel Prize for his life's work and contributions to children's literature. The book tells the story of a twelve-year-old Yemenite girl, "a dirty and starving new immigrant" whose father brings her to a veteran settler's house, seeking to hire her out as nanny for their son. At the veteran's house, Rumiah goes through a metamorphosis. First, the veteran's family changes her name to the more Hebrew name of Moriah. Then they bathe and clean her, and comb her hair. They believe, says Kipnis, that in a very short time she will become a human being, ready to learn some manners.

In the eyes of the veteran's family, Rumiah has two very

important attributes: First, her father did not ask for much money in exchange for her work. Second, she is considered better than an Ashkenazi girl, for she eats little and works much. When selling Rumiah to the veteran's wife, the matchmaker—a woman herself—explains that all Rumiah requires is a stick and a belt, "without which one could not get her moving."

I found this book at the National Book Fair in Jerusalem in 1991, searching the children's literature counter looking for books for my son. While holding this book in my hands, it occurred to me that my feelings of alienation and self-hatred were based on this exact kind of work. I had experienced and developed my negative feelings as a child when, reading this sort of literature, I believed every word. All that was Mizrahi was said to be retarded, degenerate, and primitive. As a result, I had "Ashkenazi-ized" myself—become "white." For me, doing so meant establishing a modern, progressive, *clean* identity, and destroying to its roots the identity my parents had given me. It meant rejecting everything: their history, language, values, loves, hates, pains, and joys.

My Ashkenazization was quite successful. I knew about Stockhausen's avant-garde music, as well as about a cappella—a genre of music developed in Christian countries where Ashkenazim came from. I was familiar with Mozart and his biography, long before the movie *Amadeus* came out, and I could recognize many of Bach's pieces by their Kuchel List number. I was familiar with Wimbledon games. I answered all the questions on Shmuel Rosen's radio quiz show, and I solved the *Ha'aretz* (a national newspaper) crossword puzzle with ease. My father was proud. I knew about *Yalkut Hakzavim* and was an expert *Chizbat* teller, as if I had heard the stories from my very own grandmother. Both are folk tales about Israeli pioneers and fighters, and my ability to recite them implied that I was part of a pioneer family.

Upon finishing *Rumiah, the Little Nanny,* I began a quest to acquire information on similar Israeli literature. In time, I discovered that Kipnis and Eliezer Shmuely, another famous children's author, were merely teachers. The foundations for their work were laid by the intellectual leaders of their generation.

My failure in school, it turned out, only served as proof of elaborate theses regarding my supposed backwardness, theses that flourished in the ivory towers of the Hebrew University. The Israeli intellectual elite had established a framework for all research into Israeli society. This framework was based upon the elite's construction of the desirable Israeli, which in turn was defined by what the Zionist labor movement found acceptable. Only later in life did I realize that all of my conceptions about what was desirable and detestable were based on these "scientific" cornerstones.

Israeli researchers Karl Fuerstein and M. Richel postulated the following: "The results these [Moroccan] youth have reached, during systematic examination, point to intellectual development retardation. Various non-verbal examinations conducted prove retardation of one to two years, and very often even more, in comparison with youth of similar age in Europe. Are we to interpret this as biological inferiority and to see their difficulties as an expression of lack of intellectual abilities and limitations in psycho-physiological activity?"[5]

They then promised to expand on all that related to the social and cultural factors that had special influence on my "dysfunctional development," as a means of offering useful advice for the educator faced with the task of re-educating me.

Fuerstein and Richel said that not only was I retarded, but that I lacked curiosity, that no one around me was capable even of arousing my curiosity, that I showed no interest in observation, and that I was unable to differentiate between the real and the imaginary, between the natural and the supernatural.

These researchers did not bother asking whether I lived in an imaginary world out of my own choice; they simply decided that I was incapable of living in any other reality. They talked about the depths of my consciousness without ever consulting me.

They instructed my teachers to avoid showing disrespect for my traditions and beliefs, even if these beliefs were "superstitious," because I would resist anyhow, as I was incapable of grasping abstract explanations. They said that beneath my "religious problem" lay my problematic relationship with the father figure. They said that my presence in a group might be dangerous, because of my sexual immorality, which was the result of my North African way of life and required the professional care of a psychologist.

Another respected researcher, Karl Frankenstein, addressed the question of what should be done to change my ethnic character. Since it apparently was rooted in my unconscious, Frankenstein asserted that conscious direction could not change it. "Only forces directed at the unconscious [were] likely to [do so]." I was thus to contend actively with my ethnic character.[6]

Which I did, even at the tender age of six, on both the individual and collective level. I invented the French girl from scraps of information taken from my mother, a girl who had a greater chance of being accepted. I tailored my world according to Frankenstein's measurements, but all in vain. For despite his recommendations, he was skeptical of my ability to change and, like Fuerstein, thought that my intelligence and ability to think abstractly were deficient. According to them, I was not blessed with the ability to think in terms of cause and effect, to understand the ways of the world, to distinguish between essential and nonessential, to relate to situations which "require comprehending reasons, rules, and the essence of things, and to adapt to new conditions which require quick observation of the common and the different."

In his article "On the Concept of Primitivity," Frankenstein analyzes the different kinds of primitivity known to him—"that of the child, that of the retard, that of the mentally ill, and that of the backward primitive and his deficient self-consciousness." All these types constituted "a mere introduction to [his] main subject—the analysis of the primitive mentality of the Mizrahi Jews, who [came] to [Israel] from culturally backward regions." According to Frankenstein, we primitive people lack a "self," and our world was not based in the personal. From my educators who consumed his writings, I understood that my self lacked all functional content (so help me G-d, what ever did he mean?) and that I was incapable of abstractly conceptualizing the "other" as having a "self" of her own.[7]

What it all meant for me was of no concern to Frankenstein or his colleagues. What mattered to them was "the big picture," as they were concerned with "the fate of the people of Israel."

Frankenstein's opinions infuriated Akiva Ernest Simon, another member of the club, who was the one to explicitly etch the term "primitivity" into this kind of work.[8] From there on, the debate was detached from reality and became entirely academic. My parents and I became abstract entities in this debate, guinea pigs through whom the argument was to be examined.

"The anthropocentric position [as opposed to religious, social, or national positions] calls for extreme caution and moderate pacing," Simon said, "if any possible changes are to take place in the social lives of the said immigrants"—meaning those of my parents and myself. "We have found that there are two fronts: the absorbers and the absorbed, the directors and the directed, the culturally developed and the culturally more primitive."

This argument caused Nathan Rottenstreich, yet another enlightened researcher, to state angrily that there is a basic methodological problem regarding the question, "To what extent is it possible and permissible to draw a line distinguishing between the different sides?"9

Rottenstreich claims that the unity of Israeli society is dependent on common conceptions of collective objectives and the means for achieving them. "Is there hope that such unity can be reached in the background of the present reality of the veteran settlers? A return to fundamentals is necessary, in order to merge into the lifestyle founded on the ideas of Israeli society."

The impact of Rottenstreich's words was of such consequence, being carried on by statesmen such as Ben-Gurion, that who was I to reject it? Who was I to doubt these truths? As funneled to me through the school system and society, I believed the researchers knew what they were talking about, so I conformed.

Over the years, I have come to see that the researchers' discourse functioned as a massive system of exclusion, filtering out those of us who failed the Ashkenazization test. It was a system fertilized by philosophical, literary, ethical, and educational establishment authorities. Their discourse influenced the minds of subsequent thinkers, all of whom in turn nurtured the myth of primitivity versus modernity.

Once that generation's leading thinkers had established and documented their theories through public lectures, conferences, books, and journals, a solid infrastructure existed upon which Ben-Gurion could base his definition of me as morally deficient. The educational system in which my brother, sister, and I were processed was based entirely upon these judgments.

This educational system was very much like the structure of Israeli sociology—a sociology whose primary purpose was, during its first years, to serve the government authorities in absorbing the mass immigration. The ideological and emotional proximity that the founders of Israeli sociology had to the Zionist project obscured the difference between what was academic and what was political. Even in instances of ideological disagreement, the aggressive Zionist belief in the establishment and subsequent fortification of the State forged a conceptual consensus.

In all of his research, Shmuel Eisenstadt preserves the distinction between pioneers and *olim* (immigrants). My parents, who had arrived after the establishment of the State, could not by his definition be considered pioneers. Moreover, in his opinion, they had no national identity, since they were neither secular nor modern enough to his liking. Because they were traditionally religious, they were dangerous to the Zionist enterprise.[10]

According to Eisenstadt, my parents were not capable of consciously transforming their economic/employment structure or their social and cultural life.[11] In reality, my father—a senior bank officer in Morocco—did change his "employment structure": In Israel, he worked in a cement factory and in the citrus harvest for several years. Still, he was not suitable for absorption, according to Eisenstadt's research. My father had to go through "something" metaphysical, which Eisenstadt terms "de-socialization," to be followed by "re-socialization." This entire process was related to "acquiring the new social values and attitudes . . . and required the gradual change of the *olim* groups."[12]

Eisenstadt's analysis laid on my father's shoulders the responsibility for failing to be absorbed into Israeli society—in other words, failing to assimilate. In Eisenstadt's statistics, my father was uneducated, despite his professional experience in banking; and my mother, a cum laude graduate of the Alliance Israelite, was but "another one of the illiterate Mizrahi immigrants." In Eisenstadt's eyes, it was of no value that both my parents had experienced Western culture through both the colonial city of Casablanca and the French education of the Alliance schools. Eisenstadt attributed my parents' failure at absorption to their being "unripe," to their being unable to enjoy the privileges of Israeli citizenship and utilize it for their "employment mobilization."[13]

My mother once worked as a maid in the Ashkenazi home of Yitzhak Ben-Zvi, the second president of Israel. She was fired after two days, because she turned out to be Moroccan—not Yemenite, as they had thought.

In another Ashkenazi home, my mother discovered the family did not keep kosher. In shock, she spit to the side, exclaiming "They're not Jews!" At that moment, she discovered that a deep chasm separated her from *Eretz Yisrael*—the land of Israel. *This* Israel was not the society into which she wanted to be absorbed. My mother, as opposed to my father, *chose* to "fail" at her social absorption.

Caught somewhere between my parents, I finally made my choice in favor of the rich, successful, and strong side, in favor of the winning side, in favor of Ashkenazization. The price I paid for my Ashkenazization was full alienation from my self and my identity. The price was also a feeling of contempt for my parents' helplessness in becoming more Ashkenazi.

According to the researchers, the story of my family's absorption was no more than an abstract analysis, couched in terms of pioneers versus immigrants. Two groups, two worlds; the former positive, the latter a danger to the former.

Eisenstadt evaluated Israel's absorption policy as being mostly appropriate. He saw the mistakes made along the way as a reasonable price to pay for learning a lesson.[14] I, Eisenstadt's object of research was the one who paid and is still paying this price. Neither he nor Ben-Gurion paid the price. None of their predecessors paid the price—not the Honorable Dr. "Liberator of Jerusalem" Yitzhak Rabin, not Member of Knesset (MK) Professor Naomi Chazan, not MK Yael Dayan, and not the minister of education, Amnon Rubinstein. It was I.

Today there are Power Rangers, Coca-Cola, and other such diseases. "Hey," a student of mine of Arab Jewish origin said to me, "look at me. I reached university and never experienced discrimination. Whoever wants to can make it. I don't want to deal with your problems, your parents' problems, or even my parents' problems: All of that is irrelevant to me."

It is I, and maybe one or two others like me, who spoil reality for this student and hang a dark cloud over the Israeli consciousness—which in 2003 is at most prepared to admit that once upon a time there was an ethnic problem in Israel. Dorit Rabinian, a second-generation Iranian-Israeli in her twenties, defines herself as a *"nouveau Frank"* ("Frank" being the pejorative term used to describe Moroccan Jews). She writes, "Any good Ashkenazi boy knows that love shmove—It's still better to marry 'one of ours.'"[15] As opposed to the Ashkenazi-ized Mizrahi boy who jokes with "the real thing"—Ashkenazi girls—and asserts, "I don't have a gold chain [symbolizing a working class Mizrahi]. I don't curse in Arabic, and my Benetton shirt is buttoned all the way up!" Any minute, he thinks, his skin will lighten in identification with the other side.

What are the Ashkenazi-ized supposed to do? Return to the past? Nostalgically romanticize the culture? Which culture—that of Kurdistan, of Morocco? That of today, of yesterday?

I speak Yiddish-Hebrew and think according to European cultural patterns. I breathe in Zionist ideology and out the *Reut* song[16] at a dizzying pace, and I hurt in "integration" terms—in terms of the educational reform meant to achieve the "melting pot" ethos. All of what I have described therefore is relevant today. It is relevant because the vast majority of children's literature written today is the project of European-originated people—people whom literature researcher Adir Cohen found are also responsible for the stereotypes representing the Arab child as inferior and monstrous. It is relevant because students are still exposed to the texts I quoted. It is there that they find the sources which define who is disadvantaged and why. It is in their very library that I found the books and articles.

Today, I wonder whether Frankenstein himself was not too primitive to be able to recognize me as the "other" in terms other than negative, and as having a "self of [my] own?" Were I to send Fuerstein to the Tundra Dunes with no knowledge of the language and with no skills for contending with such a way of life, would he have survived the intellectual and physical tests of such a situation? What did those researchers know about me as an "other" anyway?

My story is one primarily of oppression: traditional European oppression, colonial oppression, Western oppression, modern Zionist oppression. Inside all of this lies a shattered, confused identity which is fighting an overwhelming struggle for control over my consciousness, values, feelings, passions, and will. I am trapped in a world of mirrors. This process is one whose nature and power I still am unable to comprehend. It is not a return to my roots, nor a rehabilitation or reconstruction of identity. These words are suspicious and dangerous to my ears. One thing, though, is clear to me: Whether I am conscious of it or not, I am a product of an educational, intellectual, and economic steamroller that squashed everything and left no room for my own development outside of the distorting, Ashkenazi, Zionist, Israeli, European hegemony.

HOW THE CAMEL FOUND ITS WINGS

I passed my quarter-century mark watching the trees blur past, speeding toward my destination at Brown University. The conference, "Israeli and Palestinian Identities in the Humanities," was right up my alley, worth spending my birthday on a Greyhound bus. I had set out for the event hoping to learn more about the topic and to meet people who shared my interest in it. But what has stayed with me from that unusual birthday was an even more unusual discovery: a metaphorical camel, two elusive wings, and the inspiration to fit together the disjointed pieces of my *own* identity.

It began on the first day of the conference, when I found myself the only student among a group of professors in a dimly lit room. We were screening the Israeli film *Ha-gamal Ha-me'ofef* (*The Flying Camel*).[1] The film's heroes, an Ashkenazi-Israeli professor and a Palestinian sanitation worker, join together on a mission to restore the ruined statue of a flying camel. In reality, this camel had stood at the entrance to the international fairgrounds in Tel Aviv in the 1930s. As such, it symbolized a different epoch, a time of possibility before the battle lines were irrevocably drawn between "Arab" and "Jew."

The film was presented to us as a model of humanistic film-making, the kind of art that transforms stereotypes into individual personalities and demonstrates the redeeming possibility of friendship. It was in fact a story brimming over with comedic imagination and political goodwill, except for one significant aspect that I alone seemed to notice: The "bad guys" in the film are the dark-skinned, dark-haired, brutish, and incurably stupid members of the Angel family. With their Sephardi last name and the father's distinct Mizrahi/Sephardi accent in Hebrew, this family exemplified the stereotypically pejorative representation of Israelis with roots in North Africa and the Middle East.

The Angels possess the original wings of the flying camel, having appended them to the angel statue that hovers over their Mizrahi-style fast-food joint. The Angel family's refusal to sacrifice the wings to the professor's cause becomes the main obstacle to the camel's successful re-memberment, and by extension, to the complete re-memberment of the Palestinian Arab and Ashkenazi Jew. This scenario reflects the predominantly Ashkenazi-Israeli Labor Party conceptions of the peace process current at the time, which cast the Mizrahi/Sephardi working class (supporters of the right-wing Likud Party) in the role of the unenlightened opponents of peace. Were the Angels not so hopelessly ignorant and barbaric, they would have surely grasped the importance of the camel's re-memberment, and happily donated the wings to the professor and his Palestinian sidekick. But the Sephardi mother in the movie is fat and coarse, incapable of comprehending the lofty significance of the professor's mission; the father small, mean spirited and weasely; and his two sons big, dark, bumbling dolts who, robot-like, carry out their father's every command.

The Angels' depiction subscribes to every stereotype in the book. Yet somehow, in a movie ostensibly about the breaking down of stereotypes, this one passed unchecked. Perhaps because such depictions of Mizrahi/Sephardi are so pervasive throughout Israeli culture they are simply taken for granted. Still, I naïvely thought to myself, who would have thought that such hackneyed representations would surface at a conference of Palestinian and Israeli intellectuals?

By the end of the screening, the camel had found two new wings, and I got to thinking. I started putting my own pieces together—making my own flying camel out of the remnants of the past, borrowing missing pieces from the present, and using my imagination and willpower to try to make it all stick together. The pieces of my own American childhood, the histories that preceded it in Israel and in Iraq, and the challenges I see before me in my work are the various fragments I have been remembering and re-membering into an integral whole. I do not yet know its shape—camel, dromedary, llama, yak—but I do not care, as long as it will fly.

In "re-membering" the broken camel, the Palestinian and Israeli heroes of the movie really are piecing together the idea of coexistence, drawing on their common humanity for the glue. Such camel-mending procedures operate on the assumption that "Arab" and "Jew" are inherently disparate identities to begin with; the restoration is therefore not of the respective categories themselves, but rather, of the harmony between them. Nowhere does this restoration take into account the fracturing of identity itself, as occurred in the dismemberment of the Arab Jew—an identity ripped like a torn book.

Before this dismemberment, there were Jews who were at

one with themselves and their surroundings, who lived in places where their families had lived for hundreds or thousands of years. They had a clear sense of who they were, in relation to their own communities and in relation to their non-Jewish neighbors. I will not venture here to assess how well Jewish minorities were or were not treated in Muslim lands, as this varied by place and period, and the topic has become the subject of so much polemic in Israeli and Jewish discourses. The crux of the matter, as pertains to my dismembered camel, is that whether or not Jews in Arab lands saw themselves as "Arabs": They were Arab by way of language, culture, food, and custom; the rest is a question of semantics. While there were always religious customs and even foods that were specifically "Jewish," Jews throughout the Arab world shared traditional cultural beliefs and practices with their Muslim, and in some cases, Christian neighbors. In the twentieth century, Jewish participation in secular Arabic music, theater, literature, journalism, and cinema soared, especially in Egypt and Iraq.

But since the mass dispersion of these Jews from their lands of origin, beginning in 1948, the Arab Jew has been cleft beyond recognition. As categories of identity, we now have "Sephardim" (literally, "Spaniards"), "Edot ha-Mizrah" ("the ethnic communities of the Orient"), and more recently, "Mizrahim" ("Orientals," or "Easterners"). Arab Jews and their descendants also are now Israeli, French, American, Canadian, Mexican, British, Australian, and so on. And in the first generations to be born in Israel and the West, many individuals are of mixed heritage—half Yemenite and half Moroccan, half Mizrahi and half Ashkenazi (such as myself), or half Mizrahi and half not Jewish. How can we, the bearers of these fragmented and mixed identities, put the camel back together in a way that makes sense to us?

To answer this question for myself, I began to reflect on my own journey, beginning with my childhood in Los Angeles. I grew up knowing next to nothing of Arab Jews, Mizrahim, or flying camels. All I had heard of were "Sephardic" Jews, a group I understood to include everyone non-Ashkenazi—and as such, half of myself. I had never heard the word "Mizrahi," and I was unaware that there could be such a thing as a Jew who would call herself or himself "Arab." Back then, "Arab" and "Jew" seemed mutually exclusive.

When I was in the first grade of my Sunday school, my teacher had each student take a turn in sharing where our *bubbe* and *zayde* (Yiddish for "grandmother" and "grandfather") were from. I remember feeling confused, not knowing what a *bubbe* or *zayde* was. Once I figured out that the other kids were talking about their grandmas and grandpas, I confidently stated that my grandma and grandpa were from Baltimore, Maryland, and that my *savta* and *saba* (Hebrew for "grandmother" and "grandfather") lived in Israel but came from Iraq.

I remember feeling pride in my difference, in being the only child in the class with a *savta* and *saba,* let alone ones who came from as far away and mysterious a place as Iraq. But in verbalizing that difference, I became conscious for the first time that I was something else—more, less, other—than what my Jewish classmates were.

My father's family had left Baghdad for Israel in 1951, along with most of Iraq's Jews. I always knew that they had endured a number of painful and traumatic years in the "transit camp" tents in Sakiyya, now called Or Yehuda. In moving to Israel, they suffered a fall in socioeconomic status and dignity so severe that the majority of women and some men in the family suffered chronic depression.

I was eight years old when I first learned of this bleak fact. During a visit to Israel, we were invited to dinner by cousins in Nahariyya, near the Lebanese border. As we entered the grassy area of their backyard, we were greeted by two long banquet tables bearing piles of food whose delicious scent wafted in the light of the summer moon. I had never seen anything like it.

Behind these tables, three fleshy matrons watched us with sad smiles and dull eyes, urging us all to eat. Coming from a family of thin people, I was surprised to see such portly relations. When I asked my parents about it, they explained that these great-aunts were bloated from the medicine they took for their depression. "Why are they depressed?" I asked. "Because of the move to Israel," my parents replied, offering no concrete details.

The connection between coming to Israel and depression seemed to be something everyone took for granted, so no further explanation would be necessary. "That move finished them," my father always said. Period. And so I came to know about the trauma without really knowing anything about it, until I grew into awareness as an adult and began asking more questions. Only then did I learn how my father's eldest sister Layla, once the beauty of the family, suffered a breakdown some ten years after her arrival to Israel and never fully recovered.

Ever since that visit to Nahariyya, I have been haunted by the sight of the three dull-eyed women poised behind the tables, so anxious that we partake of their food. That food was more than the product of two straight days of cooking: It was the last hope for continuity, the sole element of their age-old culture that survived uprooting. All other vestiges of life in

Iraq, including language and culture, were swallowed into the mud of the transit camp. As for my own Iraqi identity, I received little more of an inheritance than the words "Iraq" and "Baghdad" and the special spices that go along with them. But for a curious child with family in a faraway place, even one bite of a dish with a funny-sounding name can be a starting point for a lifetime journey.

My path of self-discovery turned out to be, paradoxically, the discovery of my own absence as daughter to a 2,600-year-old Iraqi heritage—my absence from the teachings at my Hebrew school; my absence from all the books on the Middle East and Israel that I read from high school on; my absence from my college curricula in Israel and the United States. In Hebrew school, we were taught "Judaism" as if it were a monolithic tradition. If we knew of anything resembling Jewish pluralism, it was only Reform, Conservative, and Orthodox Judaism. I was not even aware that there was such as thing as *nusah Sephardi*—that there were different traditional melodies and modes of prayer among Mizrahi/Sephardi and Ashkenazi Jews—until I met religious Mizrahim and Sephardim as a young adult.

When I was seventeen, in my senior year of high school, I began nurturing my curiosity about the Middle East through reading. For a history class, I was assigned *The Middle East in World Affairs*. This book marked the beginning of my real education about Mizrahim, the education I didn't receive in the poverty-stricken "development towns" and poor Mizrahi neighborhoods of Israel, but conversely, in the seat of privilege—in a private high school and later, in the elite American Ivy League. There, as I tried to learn about the historical context of my family's experience, I encountered misconceptions and misinformation in numerous guises, in people as well as in print.

From the history book, I learned that "this hostility [between Israel and the Arab states] had another tragic consequence, namely, the uprooting of the many old and frequently prosperous Jewish communities in Arab countries. Reprisals against the Jews of Yemen led them to emigrate en masse to Israel, causing no little trouble for the new, progressive state in having to absorb a *backward, Oriental, and almost alien mass of refugees.* No contrast could be greater than between a *lice-infested, Arabic-speaking, brown-skinned, and superstitious Yemenite coolie* and a London-bred and Oxford-educated English Jew, and the latter predominated in the higher echelons of the Israeli Foreign Office (Italics mine.)"[2]

How can one explain the printing of this unmitigated vitriol? The passage appears in no less than the fourth edition of the book, printed in 1987. It reflects how Arab Jews/Mizrahim have been presented to the literate world even by the reputable Cornell University Press. And as for myself, Professor Lenczowski's totalizing distinction between Eastern Jew versus Western Jew was hardly cryptic; even at seventeen, I knew on which side of the divide my Iraqi family fell.

Some years later I also discovered my absence from Middle Eastern memory. In the summer of 1994, my sister and I took an impromptu trip from Israel to Cairo. My sister looks very Middle Eastern; as my mother says, "The map of Iraq is written all over her face." So in Cairo, many people addressed her in Arabic, which neither of us knew at the time. On the way back from seeing the pyramids at Giza, the taxi driver (actually, a moonlighting university student whose car was two breaths away from the junkyard) asked if she was an Arab.

"Our father is from Iraq," my sister offered hesitantly.

"So you are Muslim!" he exclaimed. My sister and I sent "uh-oh" glances to one another. *How are we going to get out of this one?*

"Uh, no," one of us said apologetically.

"So you are Christian, then," he deduced, sounding a tad disappointed.

"Well, no."

"Not Muslim and not Christian? What are you then?" he asked, truly perplexed.

"Actually, we're Jewish," said my sister.

"Jewish? What's that?" he asked in dismay.

At a loss, I decided to try the Hebrew term, thinking it might be similar to Arabic, and was I ever right. As soon as I said *"Yehu*dee," accent on the last syllable, the driver turned all the way around in his seat. For a second I was sure that he was going to rear-end the car in front of us, but at the last moment, he slammed on the brakes. *"Yahudee?"* he repeated, accent on the second syllable, as pronounced in Arabic. "But this is impossible! You said that your father is from Iraq."

"He is from Iraq, and he is Jewish—uh—*yahudee.*"

"But all the *yahud* come from Europe!" he insisted.

For the remainder of the trip, he refused to believe our assertion that once upon a time, not even so long ago, there were Jews all throughout the Middle East. Such ignorance is, I now believe, the joint product of decades of Arab and Israeli propaganda, both aimed at erasing Arab Jews (a category of identity and historic experience that threatens the clear distinction between "us" and "them") from the collective memory of their people. At that moment, however, it felt as though this denial were aimed directly at me. I redoubled my already-growing resolve to learn Arabic.

I did begin learning Arabic in college, and encountered even more unwillingness to question the mental and physical fences separating Hebrew and Arabic, Jew and Arab. When I told the professor of Hebrew literature in my department that I wanted to write my undergraduate honors thesis on the poetry of Anton Shammas and Na'im 'Araide (two Palestinian-Israeli writers of both Hebrew and Arabic), she refused to work with me, offering flimsy excuses.

After a few weeks of trying to meet with her and getting nowhere, I asked her bluntly: "I know there's another reason behind this. Would you tell me what the real problem is?" She paused, made a face, then answered me in Hebrew. "I feel you're neglecting your Hebrew because of this Arabic business. But I understand your attraction to Arabic—it seems more exotic to you." Those, her exact words, stung. I could not forget them even if I wanted. In Hebrew, she used the word *zar* to describe my "attraction" to Arabic. *Zar* means, in equal measure, "foreign," "exotic," "strange," "other"— in short, everything that is not "self," that is not familiar, not home.

Did this young, female, ostensibly progressive professor know that my father and his entire family were born in Iraq, that Arabic was their mother tongue, that Arabic was the language in which my grandmother expressed her love for me and my sister on our all-too-brief visits to Israel? She did. Her choice of words was not accidental.

This professor had taken me under her wing when I took two of her Hebrew poetry classes my first year at Columbia. When I divulged to her that I wanted to try my hand at writing in Hebrew she encouraged me, and we met occasionally for coffee, to look at what I had written.

Sometimes, in my verse, I quoted the slightly ironic, proverbial wisdom of my favorite aunt. In one such case, the professor contested my usage of a particular word (*shama* instead of *sham* for "there"), informing me that my family's Hebrew was "incorrect" and a bad influence on mine. "But that's the way people speak," I argued. I could hear the voice of my aunt echoing in the line I had written, and I wanted to remain faithful to it. "That doesn't matter," she told me, "it's like writing in Black English. You don't want to write or speak that way, or you won't be taken seriously. Would you write 'ain't' in a poem?" *Yes*, I thought to myself, *I would, if I were African American, and that was my writing voice*. But I said nothing, and we dropped the subject.

A year and a half later, standing at the entry to her office, I was stunned into silence. I did not know what to say that would make this professor understand how wrong she was. In the privacy of my dorm room that night, I cried. I was hotly angry, unsure of why my professor's words were so terribly upsetting to me. I still did not connect her reply to our old quibble over the word usage. Or to the reality that our relationship had been deteriorating ever since I began studying Arabic. Or to the fact that in her advanced Hebrew poetry class, all the poets were integrated into the syllabus thematically under topics such as memories of childhood or experiences of war, except for both Mizrahi and Palestinian poets—featured during one week only (out of fourteen) and pigeonholed together as *Meshorerim Mizrahim*, "(Oriental Poets)."

From my professor's syllabus, one would surmise that while Ashkenazi poets could be incorporated into a lecture called

"Mother, Father, and Jerusalem," poets like the Moroccan-Jewish Erez Bitton or the Palestinian-Arab Na'im 'Araide could not share these universal concerns. All they had to contribute to any discussion of Hebrew writing was their ethnicity. I suppose that I should have been grateful that they were included at all, as most such college curricula would exclude them altogether.

I carried out my project without my professor's help, and it won the department's award for the best honors thesis that year. During the months I spent working on it, I even had dreams in which I confronted my professor with the words that had not come to me during that moment outside her door; for I finally understood why she had "no time" to advise me—a senior in her department—on poetry written in the language she taught. Had I begun to show an interest in learning Yiddish, rather than Arabic, I have no doubt her response would have been different. But she "understood" my grievous error, really understood why I was investing so much time in learning this "other, exotic, foreign" language, as opposed to one that was clearly, inarguably, my "own." I never confronted her, and to this day I doubt she could imagine how deeply she affected me.

Scenarios like these form my camel's legs, head, and hump. Had I only learned through bad examples, I probably would have an ordinary, terrestrial camel. But fortunately, I also benefited from positive knowledge, blessing my camel with wings. In college, for example, I befriended Arab and other Middle Eastern graduate students and scholars who not only knew about Middle Eastern Jews, but were well-informed about Mizrahim in Israel, and took an interest in me. Over the course of many long conversations, I began to develop an awareness of the points of contact between us—our family histories and our experiences as the first generation to straddle the divide between East and West.

Those ideas were augmented during a year I spent in Jerusalem working in the media and studying at the Hebrew University. There I met student activists passionately concerned with the same social, cultural, and academic issues I had begun exploring. They were members of Tsedek Hevrati (Social Justice), a student organization devoted to activism on behalf of Mizrahim and other disempowered sectors in Israel. Many of them had experienced outright discrimination and some of them, poverty. Their formative experiences were doubtless much harsher than mine, yet they took my own agendas and interests quite seriously. I learned a tremendous amount from these formidably intelligent and intensely committed students. As I participated in the group's activities and initiated some events on my own, I finally found the confidence to begin re-membering the Arab-Jewish camel aloud.

With those invaluable experiences fresh in my mind, I returned to the States to start graduate school at UC Berkeley. There I set about gaining the textual knowledge necessary for re-memberment on not just a personal, but an academic level, for filling in gaps and creating an alternative to Lenczowski's "Yemenite coolie." Yet even then, I continued to derive much from direct experience. When the director of an intensive summer Arabic program at Middlebury College in Vermont told me that he did not and would not accept the principle of "Arab Jew," I argued with him. He agreed with me that "Arab" is a matter neither of religion nor of nationality, but of cultural and linguistic affiliation and identity. He nonetheless insisted that while a Jew can be Egyptian, Syrian, Iraqi, and so forth, s/he simply cannot be called "Arab."

Half of the faculty members (all of them Muslim and Christian Arabs, from several countries) joined in the argument, some arguing my case, some the director's. I mentally took a step back in the midst of the clamor, amazed that I had instigated such an impassioned discussion about a principle of identity that seemed to matter to everyone there, across the spectrum of our religions and nationalities. I realized how far I had come since my twenty-fifth birthday some two and a half years earlier.

Indeed, when I look back on all those moments, I am struck both by how distant they seem and by how much they must have directed my life's path. I see them now from the vantage point of a student who has spent five years working toward a Ph.D. on the literature of Arab Jews, from that of a Jewish woman who has spent a year living in Cairo, who has visited synagogues in Syria and who even made it, in June 2002, to Baghdad for one week. Each of those experiences could easily become an essay in itself. But what I think is most important to describe here is the process that initiated, motivated, and in fact enabled them.

Back then, when the movie about the flying camel was over, I wanted to say something, to make the others see what I had seen. I wish I could report that I raised my concerns in the brief discussion that followed or in the conference's round-table closing remarks. But I did not. Even when the professor cosponsoring the conference praised the film's merits, I kept quiet.

I knew my protest would require an explanation that I felt neither confident enough nor equipped to provide. In addition, I thought it would be inappropriate to ruin good intentions with nitpicky criticisms coming from left field. I had not yet connected my Hebrew professor's remarks to the depiction of the most un-angelic Angel family, and I had not yet connected either with the esteemed Professor Lenczowski's description of the "lice-infested, Arabic-speaking, brown-skinned, and super-stitious Yemenite coolie."

I now string all these experiences together and recognize that they were neither isolated nor minor incidents. While discrimination, ignorance, and misunderstanding come in all shapes, sizes, and colors, including that called "best intentions," they remain, at the end of the day, discrimination, ignorance, and misunderstanding. The same one-dimensional, unintelligent stereotypes and assumptions appeared in a Cornell University Press text, a poetry class at Columbia, a movie shown at a conference held at Brown. In passing through the intellectual filters of American universities, these misperceptions of Mizrahi- and Sephardi-Israelis are institutionalized, legitimized, and disseminated as self-evident facts.

I feel the problem stems, first of all, from a total blindness to its very existence. The professor who informed me I was learning Arabic because it was more exotic to me than Hebrew certainly would not consider herself racist, prejudiced, or, G-d forbid, ignorant. After all, she had taken pains to include those "Oriental Poets" in her syllabus. Likewise, the professors who co-organized the conference at Brown would have been mortified had I pointed out the flaws of their humanistic film. They meant well; clearly, it had just not occurred to them to look *beyond* the representations of Arab and Jew, to see *what kind* of Arab, *what kind* of Jew, and as follows, what kind of message.

Even after one recognizes that the "Arab Jew" camel is broken and missing its wings, the camel remains dis-membered. How, then, to re-member it? I feel the solution is highly individual, resistant to generalizing prescriptions, for there is no return to a lost collective past. Nostalgia for "authenticity" can be a self-defeating mechanism: Mizrahim today are not what our parents were and definitely not what our grandparents were. Nor would I, for one, want the traditional lifestyle of my grandmother. Like it or not, we are hybrids of past and present, old and new, East and West. The restored camel must, by definition, become something other than what it once was. Our Arab Jewish origins remain elusive, and stone camels, with all the best intentions, cannot always be made to fly.

Fortunately, identities are highly portable. We can attempt to re-member ourselves into integral, whole people, the rightful owners of our pasts and futures, regardless of where we now live—Be'er Sheva, Paris, Long Island, or Montreal. Our identities, perhaps the only thing truly our own, can be fashioned as we ourselves choose, paving a unique path to our future—a path that is part inheritance and part creativity, baseline and improvisation.

For me, re-membering my identity entails learning Arab Jewish history, languages, and culture. My curiosity about Jewish life in the Arab world only grows greater as I learn more. The impulse that drives me is not that of the curator, seeking to put these fragments behind a protective glass, but that of the artist, seeking to bring them into dialogue with the dynamic, living present. I am moved to create something that is new, yet part of a continuum of cultural development.

Arab Jewish culture may seem like a fading remnant of the lost past. But Arabic cultures of all kinds have been negotiating with the forces of modernization and globalization that affect local cultures everywhere. We may never know what our grandparents knew by way of so many things—jokes, stories, proverbs, rituals, songs—but the possibilities for energetic cultural renewal, emphasizing a fusion of who we are and who "we" were, are great.

My identity, then, is an ever-evolving creation. I was born with the various parts, some through immediate circumstance and some by dint of heritage, but I and only I can locate them, reclaim them, and decide how to fit them together. I am in a continuous process of learning, correcting, and refining, as I search for the remaining pieces of my own flying camel. Whether or not it flies, whether or not it even resembles a camel, I hope to put together something that can take me across the shifting sands of my memories, desires, and dreams.

Secrets

My great-grandfather was the famous Hakim Yahya, a respected physician in the city of Kashan and one of the few educated and licensed physicians in Iran. The descendant of a family of *hakims*, he had a great knowledge of Eastern medicine and the use of herbs.

After Yahya's wife, Hayat, gave birth to their fourth daughter, the couple's family not only hoped for but expected a son. With intense pressure from his wife and others, Yahya put together an ancient herbal formula for helping give birth to a boy. Up to that point, he had resisted his wife's demands to mix up the formula, because it was known to have dangerous side effects. But after the birth of his fourth daughter, even he was convinced that no son would be born to his family without some help.

The formula was proven successful by the birth of my grandfather, and demands for this miracle potion skyrocketed among those who heard about it. Many people begged Yahya to let them use the herbal drink—couples who were desperate to have sons, because they had "too many" daughters; couples who had sons but wanted more; and women who wanted to avoid the evil tongue and gossip of their in-laws, as well as the cold shoulders of their husbands, should they not produce sons during their first pregnancies. Yahya had difficulty convincing these people of the dangers that went along with the formula—dangers enhanced by its improper use in the hands of eager parents-to-be. Nonetheless, he did mix up the formula for three couples whom he deemed either worthy or desperate. The first two couples followed Yahya's strict directions, and the women gave birth to healthy boys without suffering any major side effects or complications. The third couple, however, had a different outcome.

The man was one of Yahya's good friends. After the birth of the couple's fifth daughter, the couple wanted a son. They were so eager to use the formula that they used more than the prescribed amount. The result was a healthy son but a mother who did not live to see her boy's first birthday, as a result of kidney failure and other complications.

After this incident, Yahya decided to destroy the formula, so nobody ever again would suffer such a loss. His wife was the only one who never forgave him for destroying it. Through its use, she had given birth to three sons, one after the other. But without the formula, she gave birth to another daughter. Fearing even more girls in the family, she refused to have any more children.

My mother's family rarely speaks of this incident, but it hovers over us whenever a daughter is born. On these occasions, the reactions of my mother's older family members—especially the women—reveal how humiliating it must have been to be born a girl or to give birth to one in Kashan. Sadly, my mother was born and raised in this kind of atmosphere.

My father's family, however, was from Hamedan, where Jews were not as negatively affected by the birth of a daughter. Jewish families in Hamedan would feel disappointed or even angry, but they would not feel panicked or desperate. My mother thinks the special hostility Kashan's Jews showed toward daughters had many psychological factors, deeply rooted in the geography of the city.

Kashan is located on the outskirts of Qom, a city with Muslim holy sites. Jews of Kashan, as well as Jews in other areas near Muslim holy sites, were under constant pressure from the local Muslim clergy to convert. Many Jews had to pretend they were converts in public, though they still followed Jewish laws at home. In addition, Jews often were forced to marry off their daughters to powerful Muslim leaders and clergy, in order to prove respect for Islam. As a result, many Jewish families arranged marriages for their daughters while the girls were very young, to avoid forced marriage to non-Jews—a fate considered to be the greatest disgrace for families.

My mother's explanation of the Kashan Jewish community's attitude toward daughters is not hard to accept, though their hostility still feels unfair and difficult to stomach. Regardless, I respect my mother for trying to make some sense and bring some logic into a reality that must have felt so senseless and illogical. Given that she was born and raised in an environment hostile to girls, given that she was around people who believed her very existence to be a disgrace to the family, her compassion for the situation is no less than inspirational.

Times do change, and with the birth of my first child, a girl, everyone was ready to share in my joy of having a baby. My parents were extremely happy. A few older aunts did not come to visit me in the hospital, never paying special visits to those giving birth to girls. They did attend the naming ceremony and celebration we had, however, bringing gifts for my daughter. But even then, they told others that such a celebration was quite unnecessary.

Five years later, I was pregnant with my second child, and my many ultrasounds and sonograms showed another girl on the way. When my parents received the news, they smiled and gave me their blessing. They agreed it would be wonderful to have two daughters—two sisters, friends for life.

My sister-in-law, on the contrary, looked disappointed. She was upset with me for not wanting to try for a third child immediately, in the hopes of finally having a boy. She told me about a new diet that would increase my chances. Maybe, I thought to myself, my great-grandfather did not truly succeed in destroying that formula after all. But I was happy, my husband was happy, and above all, my daughter anxiously was waiting for the birth of her little sister and playmate.

A week before my due date, I experienced some complications, and my doctor decided to have another, more accurate sonogram done. This time the radiologist informed me, with a big smile on his face, that I was having a boy. Somehow he had mistaken the baby's sex in the four previous sonograms.

The reality of having a boy instead of a girl brought forth many different and unexpected reactions from my family: My father, who up until then had wished for a healthy baby above all, ran inside the house to kiss me and give me a huge hug. He had not reacted that way to the birth of my first daughter or to the announcement I was having another one. My mother looked relieved but tried to hide her excitement.

My husband, who had told me how he wanted only daughters, got tears in his eyes. My older brother cheered loudly and said how much better it was to have a boy. "Especially since you already have a girl," he added as an afterthought. My sister-in-law was delirious with excitement. And finally I got a call from two of the older aunts who had not even congratulated me after the birth of my daughter. "I heard your baby is a boy," they said. "May he be healthy, and G-d bless your family!" The only ones who were still in shock and still wanted a little girl (especially after looking at all the beautiful girl clothes I had bought or received as gifts) were my sister, my daughter, and me.

The last week of pregnancy went by very fast. My son was born at 10:30 P.M., and by 9:00 A.M. the next morning, visitors and well-wishers had crowded my hospital room. It had been much easier to feed and change my daughter when she was born, because there were not so many people around me. But my baby was a healthy and beautiful child, and I felt as happy as when my daughter was born.

My parents and husband decided to have a big party for the *brith milah*, and it was a joyous occasion. I could not help but notice, however, that the light beaming from my father's eyes, the pride filling my mother's eyes, and the broad smile covering my brother's face had not been there during my daughter's naming celebration. I thought we had come so far in my generation, in our attitudes toward girls. Until that moment, I did not realize that being born a girl or a boy would still make a difference in my family.

When my father carried my little son to put in the rabbi's arms, the rabbi started chanting the *bracha*, and his beautiful voice filled the room. Everyone became quiet. As I looked around the room into the eyes of the many women who had gathered to celebrate and share in our happiness, I thought of the stories hidden behind each of those eyes.

Across from me, Farideh Khanoum sat next to her seven-teen-year-old son. She had become friends with my mother exactly nine months before his birth. She was only six years older than my mother, but she looked many years my mother's senior. I remembered the day we met her. I had accompanied my mother to her gynecologist, to find out if she was pregnant with my younger brother. Farideh Khanoum came out of the examination room with a panic-stricken look on her face, visibly shaking and distraught. She did not leave the office, but sat on a chair in the waiting room and wept.

My mother and I were shocked. It crossed my mind that the doctor must have given her some horrible news about her health. Since she looked 100 percent Iranian, my mother approached her and started talking to her in Farsi. Farideh Khanoum looked at my mother with tears in her eyes. She started shaking her head as she answered my mother. *"Chi begam khanoum . . .* What can I say? How will I be able to explain this to people? I am disgraced. How can I ever hold my head up among family and friends again?" She rocked her body back and forth, like a child in pain. "What is wrong?" my mother asked. "Nothing can be this bad. G-d is always with you in bad situations. Tell me, maybe I can help."

After some minutes of silence, as though trying to collect her thoughts, Farideh Khanoum asked my mother if she was Jewish. "Yes, I am the daughter of Aziz from Kashan. Do you know the family?" My mother replied immediately, trying to put the woman's mind at ease and make some possible con-nection with her. Farideh Khanoum smiled. She said that she heard many good things about the family and that she was friendly with my mother's cousin. The connection made her feel close enough to confide in my mother.

"The doctor just informed me that I am pregnant!" she exclaimed. She sighed and started rocking again.

"Well, that is wonderful!" my mother tried in a cheery voice. "Babies are a blessing from G-d!"

"No, *khanoum joon* (dear lady), you don't know what a disaster this is. I have three daughters, and my eldest is engaged to be married in two weeks. How can I go around being pregnant, with three grown daughters and a son-in-law? *Khodaya cheh konam* (oh G-d), what should I do?" she cried.

"How old are your daughters?" my mother asked. "My eldest is twenty-four; she is engaged," Farideh Khanoum replied. "My second daughter is twenty, and my youngest is eighteen. So you see, there is no way I can have a child now, with a daughter engaged and two grown daughters ready for marriage. Oh, the shame of it all!" Farideh Khanoum wept again and put her head on my mother's shoulder, relieved to tell someone what she had been through. In between her tears, she pulled back, shook her head, and talked.

"My daughter got engaged six months ago. Ever since then, my son-in-law spends the night at our house every *Shabbat*. It is a tradition—a stupid tradition if you ask me—what for? My husband used to do the same back in Iran." She continued in a bitter and sad voice. "I was only fourteen when we got engaged. He wanted to touch me and get close to me at night, when everyone was sleeping. We all slept in the same room. Oh G-d, I was so ashamed, but I couldn't talk or scream—I would wake up my parents. *Khodaya,* the shame of it!"

Farideh Khanoum went on to explain how her husband had insisted that their son-in-law follow the same *Shabbat* tradition and spend Friday nights at their house. "He probably was reminded of his own courting and flirting and thought it would be fun for our son-in-law. I have to say, my daughter enjoys her fiancé's presence far more than I did my husband's. I was so young; I hardly even knew him. I had no idea what went on between a man and a woman. It is a crime to raise girls without any such knowledge."

Farideh Khanoum painfully recounted how her husband had demanded sex from her on one of the nights when their son-in-law was present. She was not ready for it. Her husband started to raise his voice and use foul language in order to have his way. "What could I do, *khanoum joon?*" Her face flushed with shame and anger. "If I did not submit, he would have raised hell! He is capable of it. And with our future son-in-law sleeping in the next room . . . We live in a three-bedroom, a small apartment. We can hear each other's snoring from the other rooms . . . Oh G-d, *khodaya,* what can I do? I will die of shame! I am too old for this!" Farideh Khanoum could not stop crying. My mother tried hard to convince her that at her age, which was only forty-three, many American women give birth to their first child.

Farideh Khanoum revealed that after her marriage at fourteen, she was unable to get pregnant for two years, maybe because her body had not yet matured. Her seeming sterility fueled much gossip, disgracing her family and giving her husband and in-laws a reason to constantly put her down and publically humiliate her. When she finally did get pregnant, she suffered two miscarriages. To make matters worse, her only successful births were to three girls. After the third, her husband became physically cold toward her and blamed her for being "physically retarded," unable to bear him sons.

"How am I going to explain this to my family?" Farideh Khanoum cried. "I wish I had the courage to walk into the doctor's office and have an abortion right now!" "Farideh Khanoum," my mother replied, "children are blessings. Don't ever talk that way. Maybe this one will be a boy, and you will finally be able to look at your in-laws with pride!" With this last remark, my mother smiled, as we both saw a gleam of hope appear in Farideh Khanoum's eyes. She stopped crying, looked at my mother, and with a trace of hope in her voice said, "Do you really think it's possible? After all these years?" "Why not?" my mother asked encouragingly.

Since that day, my mother and Farideh Khanoum have been close friends. Farideh Khanoum broke the news of her pregnancy to her family after her daughter's wedding. To her surprise, her daughters and son-in-law were supportive of her. Not to her surprise, her husband only gave her a scornful smile. Nine months later, some weeks before the birth of my younger brother, she gave birth to her son. Her husband wanted to throw a big party for the *brith milah;* but at Farideh Khanoum's insistence and with her son-in-law's intervention, they had a small gathering instead.

As the rabbi continued his heavenly chant for my son, Farideh Khanoum took her own son's arm and gazed at him with tearful eyes. For the first time, I deeply felt the pain she had endured; and at that moment, I realized more than ever the deep-rooted humiliation an Iranian Jewish woman suffers when she is unable to bear a son.

A couple of seats to the right of Farideh Khanoum, my mother's elderly aunt sat in an armchair. *Ameh joon* Esther, dear Aunt Esther, lived in a convalescent home. Her son, Hooshang, had brought her to see the ceremony, with the understanding that he would take her back to the convalescent home that night. Given her age and condition, taking care of Ameh Esther was not easy, and her daughter-in-law, Souri, did not want to be stuck with her overnight.

Iranian Jewish tradition dictates that parents live out the remainder of their lives in the home of their eldest son. Souri, however, managed to convince Hooshang that a convalescent home would be better for Ameh Esther, given her condition. Many times in family women's gatherings, Souri had said, "After all she has done to me—the things she has said behind my back, the things she has said against my family—she now expects me to take care of her and tend to her every whim. This is not Iran, and I am not my poor mother, who suffered all her life in company of my grandmother. Thank G-d that I do not have a son; I never will be labeled 'The Husband's Mother.'"

Ameh Esther was Hakim Yahya's fourth daughter, four years older than my grandfather. I looked at her during the ceremony and gazed into her eyes—cold eyes void of feeling, staring aimlessly forward—the eyes of a woman who had been through so much in life that nothing seemed to matter anymore. As she began to shake her head slowly up and down, I remembered the big party given in honor of my cousin's *brith milah*, twenty years earlier.

Ameh Esther, strong and healthy back then, seated herself at the kitchen table to help my grandmother set up for dinner. As usual, my grandmother would not let her touch anything, out of respect for her place in the family. So Ameh Esther sat there with nothing to do, seemingly reluctant to join the happy chatter of the party in the other room. I sensed she was looking for an excuse to pour out her heart.

"This is nothing," she said proudly and grudgingly, addressing my mother. "It's a very small party compared to the one my Nasser [her youngest son] threw for the birth of his son. They had two different caterers. Do you remember?" My mother nodded, said something nice about that party, just to shut her up, and continued pouring white rice into a big serving dish. But that did not stop Ameh Esther. It really did not matter who was listening to her; she just needed to talk, to share her pain.

After a short pause, she looked at me, as if she had just remembered the source of that pain. "I remember your grandfather's *brith milah.* I was four years old when your grandfather was born. It was such an exciting day—everyone was running around, celebrating. You could not recognize my mother's face; she was smiling, joking with the servants. My three sisters and I were left in our room to entertain ourselves." Ameh Esther told her story in a tone laced with wonder, sadness, and pain.

"The *naneh,* our maid and nanny, forgot to give us breakfast. She had no time to listen to our pleas of hunger, even though it was long past lunch. Finally my older sister, who was eight, went to the kitchen, which was all the way at the end of the garden and down many steps. We were not allowed to go there. She went anyhow and brought back some bread and cheese . . ." Ameh Esther paused and looked at me. Tears welled in her eyes, but she smiled. "Everyone was so happy about the birth of your grandfather, they forgot all about us."

"Were you happy?" I asked, not realizing what great wounds I was ripping open. She looked at me with a scornful smile. "Of course. The first son after the four of us . . ." She paused again. After a few seconds, she started talking as though deep in a trance.

"My parents threw a big party for his *brith milah*. Everyone was there, dressed in their finery, but my sisters and I did not attend. Nobody had cared to ask Molouk Khanoum, the tailor, to make us dresses for the party. As soon as my mother saw us in our regular dresses, she screamed that we looked miserable and said we better not show our faces at the party, or she would die of shame. I liked the thought of a new baby, but from the start it was like my brother was the only living creature in the house. My dad did not even have time to hug me anymore. So I hated my brother. As the days passed, I hated him more and more—"

Ameh Esther stopped abruptly, as though just realizing what she had said. She looked around in a panic. No one was listening to her, except me. She stared at me, trying to figure out whether I heard or understood what she had said. "Why did you hate my grandfather?" I asked curiously. A nervous smile covered her lips. "Well you know," she said, "all children hate the baby of the house. He gets all the attention. Your grandfather was very beautiful, so he got even more attention—"

Despite Ameh Esther's obvious discomfort, I could not help persisting with questions. I had to know why she hated my grandfather, especially considering all he did for her. I knew that after the death of her first husband, when she was a very young widow with five children, he was the only person who supported her. For many years, he helped with her legal, financial, and emotional problems. He also found her a suitable second husband—a man who cared for her children as if they were his own, a man who was kind and respectful to her. So why would she hate such a wonderful brother?

"So what did you do?" I asked, trying to dig as deep as an eleven-year-old can. She waved her hand, gave a small laugh, and said, "Oh, nothing. I used to wake him up sometimes from his nap, when he was a baby. You know—all the mischievous little pranks kids play on each other." She looked around to see whether any of the grownups were hearing her remarks.

I tried to get to the root of the matter with a different approach. "How old were you when your first husband passed away?" I thought this question would remind Ameh Esther of my grandfather's many virtues. She looked at me in shock and disbelief, not expecting such a forward question from a little girl. Suddenly her eyes sparkled, as she recognized the opportunity to change the subject. "I was very young when he passed away, but do you know how old I was when I married him?" I shook my head, and she asked my age. "Eleven," I replied. Ameh Esther smiled at me. "I was ten years old when I married. A year younger than you are." In a loud voice, she continued, "Have you gotten your period yet?"

The shoe was on the other foot, and it was my turn to be embarrassed and nervous. As though her question had hit the exact target, my mother raised her head from arranging oven-roasted chicken on a silver platter and answered for me. "No, *Ameh joon,* she has not."

"Well," Ameh Esther said to my mother, "did you know that the first time I got pregnant, I was only eleven years old, and I had not gotten my first period yet?" This remark finally got the attention of all who were helping out in the kitchen—except my grandmother, who probably had heard the tale many times before.

Ameh Esther continued with pride, "I was still a child, G-d knows. I remember every morning after my husband left for work, I went outside and played with the neighborhood children in the street. One day, as usual, I was playing and jumping rope with another girl, when all of a sudden I felt sick and started bleeding . . ." Ameh Esther stopped. She had started the story with enthusiasm and excitement in her voice, but tears began welling in her eyes. She straightened her body and fingered her headscarf.

"What happened then, *Ameh joon?*" my mother asked after a long silence. *Ameh* Esther turned tear-filled eyes towards my mother and shrugged her shoulders. "I fainted," she said remorsefully. "They took me home and called the midwife and my father. They said I had been pregnant and had a miscarriage. You see, I did not know that I was pregnant. I had not gotten my first period yet. I was a child."

"How sad," I commented. I had just found out about intercourse and about how babies were made. The thought of having to go through the pain of sex and pregnancy at that age seemed so horrible that it repulsed me. "Yes, it was very sad," Ameh Esther replied sorrowfully. "Some time later, the rabbi informed me that such a child would have had a special position within the Jewish community from a religious standpoint, especially if it had been a boy."

Twenty years later, looking at Ameh Esther from across the room, I understood why she had not found the act of intercourse, forced on a ten-year-old girl, to be as sad as the fact that her baby, perhaps a boy, had been miscarried due to her childish play. A grandson with special community status would have made Ameh Esther's parents realize that she existed. It would have bestowed pride on her and her family, compensating them all for the shame she had brought as the fourth daughter in a row. I finally felt the pain in *Ameh joon* Esther's heart. I knew that if I were in her shoes, I would hate my brother, too. I would not care how nice or caring he was as an adult.

The ceremony continued. As the rabbi put the wine-soaked piece of gauze into my baby's mouth, my friend Nahzee entered the room. Nahzee and I had met in an English class during our first year in university. The teacher had asked us to choose a topic for an essay, and she had chosen to write about Iran, thus catching my attention. As it turned out, we had many friends in common, and we both had migrated from Iran one year before the Revolution. We became very good friends in a short time.

Nahzee had an Eastern beauty that attracted the attention of many boys in and out of school. She never wore any makeup, and despite all the attention, she seemed oblivious to her own attractiveness. Her main goal in life was to study and become a doctor. At our first meeting, she told me how happy she was to continue with her studies. She did not want to be married, like her sisters, before even having her high school diploma. Her two older sisters had been married in Iran before the age of eighteen. She also had an older brother and a younger sister, both unmarried. She was thankful to her brother for supporting her desire to get a higher education, like the one he received. He had convinced their father that having a college degree is important in today's society, even for a girl. "If my brother is in a good mood when I talk to him," Nahzee confided, "and if he agrees with me, he can change our father's opinion about anything. But you have to be very respectful when you talk to him. After all, he is the only son."

During the first three years of college, Nahzee was full of life and energy. She took more than fifteen units per semester, worked at a lab after school, and worked as a pharmacist's assistant during the summer. I truly admired her for the way she studied and worked to reach her goal. Biology was a very challenging and competitive major, yet she maintained a 3.8 average. Nahzee had a real passion for medicine and knew exactly where she was headed. She always talked about her dream of becoming a pediatrician, because she loved children. She looked forward to being accepted to a good medical school.

Through the years, she turned down many suitors, all of them among the most eligible bachelors in the Iranian-Jewish community. She complained that none of them wanted to be a doctor's husband, that they discouraged her dreams and goals. "Most Iranian men," she said, "feel intimidated by a woman who has a higher education than them, feel insecure around a woman who is smarter than they are. I am sure that when I am a doctor, no Persian man even will want to date me."

Nahzee's family, especially her father, was not happy about the way she turned down all her suitors. After a certain age, a young woman is considered a spinster, and having spinster daughters in the house is disgraceful among family and friends.

In the beginning of our fourth year, Nahzee was very excited, as well as anxious, about sending applications to different medical schools. But her father altogether opposed the idea of her becoming a doctor, and her brother forbade her from moving to another city to attend school. One day, toward the end of the year, I saw her in the cafeteria. Her eyes were red and puffy, making it clear she had been crying for a long time. I rushed to her side and asked what happened.

As tears once again welled in her big brown eyes and rolled down her smooth, olive skin, she explained how she had always hoped that her father and brother would finally agree with her decision to attend medical school. "I thought that once my brother saw how good my grades were; once he saw that I could take care of myself and work and study, he would let me go. But I was wrong." Nahzee tried to convince her family that she would not let medical school interfere with getting married, that she would become a loving mother and obedient wife. She promised she would not show off her education and promised that if her husband did not wish her to continue studying or working, she would quit at once.

Nahzee's family, like many other Iranian-Jewish families, believed that a woman doctor would be an instant turnoff for men. Back then, I felt that her parents were exaggerating. I thought the Iranian-Jewish men of our generation would be more liberal, that they would want to marry educated women and would not feel threatened by the extent of that education. Little did I know that the majority of these men were raised and taught by parents who felt the same as Nahzee's. As such, years later, my friends with doctorates had a major challenge finding mates who would be proud of, or even accept, their wives' achievements.

Nahzee tried hard, but she was not able to convince her family. They told her to abandon the thought of medical school at once. During her fifth and senior year, she rarely showed up at the library for the study sessions. She increased her work hours and tried to spend less time at home. By the end of the year, her grade point average had dropped from 3.8 to 3.0. We graduated together in the spring, but I rarely saw or heard from her after that. Through mutual friends, I did find out that Nahzee was working fulltime at the pharmacy and taking revenge on her parents by refusing to see any of her suitors after the first date.

Two weeks before the birth of my son, Nahzee called me out of the blue to invite me to her wedding. I had not seen or heard from her in three years, and I was overjoyed with the news. She sounded happy on the telephone. Her fiancé was a lawyer; they had met at a friend's house. She was planning to quit her job at the pharmacy to attend paralegal classes, so she could help her husband. When I called Nahzee back to invite her to my son's *brith milah,* she said, "Great! It's a boy, so he can go to school anywhere he chooses, right?"

As she walked into the room on the day of my son's party, her beauty was the same as it had been ten years before, but the sparkle in her big brown eyes and the passion of her spirit were gone. I prayed for G-d to bless her with many children, but especially a daughter. I knew her daughter would never be restricted from or limited in pursuing her life's ambition.

Finally, my son was handed to me—a helpless, beautiful, innocent little being, who needed my unconditional love and attention. A precious little human, whom I loved with all my heart and soul. I was responsible for him and proud of him—not because he was a boy, but because he was my child. I took the baby, held my daughter's little hand in mine, and asked her, "Would you please come and help me take care of our little baby?" She gave me a big smile, put her lips on her brother's hand, and kissed it. With pride blooming from her eyes she said, "Sure."

WE ARE HERE AND THIS IS OURS

a personal report on the first feminist conference for Mizrahi/Sephardi and Ethiopian-Jewish women, "Anahnu Kan Veze Shelanu (We Are Here and This Is Ours)" May 17–19, 1996, Netanya, Israel.

The "I" word: Identity. Who am I?

I knew the answer in relation to the world in which I was raised—a world constantly defined by people who did not represent me: I was a feminist in a patriarchal reality, an Iraqi in an American reality, a Mizrahi in an Ashkenazi reality, a Jew in an Arab reality. I knew very well who I was in contrast to others, but I was not quite sure how I fit in with those who shared all my identities. So the idea of a conference for Mizrahi feminists was a bit heady.

When the conference organizers asked me to submit a proposal for leading a workshop, I was thrilled. Then I was terrified. I suddenly felt inadequate. I found myself wondering what I could possibly have to say to Mizrahi women, what I could possibly contribute that Mizrahi women did not already know. Thus began the search for my place in the newly forming Mizrahi feminist community.

My issue-oriented work, I realized, was geared towards the Ashkenazi establishment. It was designed to bust down the walls of Eurocentric exclusion, and it was aimed at raising consciousness of the struggles and heritage of non-European Jews. It covered the basics: We exist, we are valid, and you need to pay attention to us. It was not, I knew, what I would want to say to a group of Mizrahi feminists.

What *would* I want to say? Things I never had been able to say to any other group of people, because nobody would have understood. Things that were buried so deep in my gut, I did not even have the words for them. I would have to remember the woman struggling inside me—the one whose Judeo-Arabic name people always botched, the one whose Mizrahi Hebrew accent[1] Jews always ridiculed, the one who wanted to sing Iraqi *Sh'bahoth* but could not find anyone with whom to sing them.

I decided that for the time being, I would fall back on a sure bet: teaching Mizrahi and Sephardi *Sh'bahoth*. Mizrahi and Sephardi women hardly ever learned these songs, so I could make an important contribution, and teaching songs would automatically create an interactive atmosphere, the perfect format for a workshop.

For various reasons, the workshop did not work out. The conference organizers, however, invited me to lead *Sh'bahoth* during the Friday night meal. As I prepared song sheets, I was relieved not to have to transliterate the Hebrew because the women would be Israeli. With no existing English transliterations of Mizrahi and Sephardi songs, I always went through the hassle of transliterating songs myself so that those who did not speak Hebrew could sing along.

I was also excited at the prospect of teaching songs I never taught Ashkenazim, some of which were my favorites. The women at the conference, I reasoned, could pick up the more complex tunes quickly, as they would already be familiar with Mizrahi and Sephardi melodic lines.

On the day of the conference, I entered the doors of the Green Beach Hotel. I drank in the images of the dark-skinned women around me. "These are Jewish women," I said to myself. "We are not all from Europe."

It did not matter that my Jewish family was from Iraq, with various shades of olive and brown skin, and that I taught about global Jewish communities. Growing up in the States, where all images of Jews were light-skinned (blond, wherever possible), with hardly any dark-skinned Jews around me to visually challenge these images, I frequently questioned myself whenever I talked about Jews of color.

In the evening, everyone sat down to eat *hamin,* Moroccan *Shebbath* stew. Most of the Ethiopians sat together at their own tables, and I was surprised by the voluntary separation between the Mizrahi/Sephardi and Ethiopian women. It seemed too much like my high school, where most of the African-American kids hung out by themselves, away from everyone else, and kids from other backgrounds did not join them. This separation jarred my image of strong Mizrahi/Sephardi–Ethiopian alliance and unity in Israel.

I asked if I could join one of the tables of Ethiopian women, and they welcomed me. As we ate, I asked typical small-talk questions, and they answered, but nobody asked me questions about myself. They spoke in Amharic to each other, and I did not understand a word. Because I did not want to spend my meal feeling alienated, between courses, I changed tables and sat with Mizrahi/Sephardi women.

Same story. I asked everyone questions, and they asked me nothing in return. They seemed uninterested in getting to know me, and I had a growing sense that it was because I was American. I suspected that I was seen as not fully legitimate, as if I were in the wrong place.

I wanted to cry: I was an outsider again. I had worked hard at soliciting funds so I could afford the trip, even though it had felt humiliating to have to ask for money. Then I had flown 10,000 miles across the world, just to feel yet again that I did not belong?

At dessert time, I picked up my belongings from the table of Ethiopian women. They asked me where I had gone, and I told them I had not understood anything they were saying, so I left. They invited me to sit back down and promised to speak in Hebrew. I sat down, and they asked me questions about myself. I felt better.

After dessert, the conference leaders told me not to lead the *Shebbath* songs. Time was too short, one of the organizers told me. I was upset, though I did not say much. I had spent a lot of time putting the song sheets together and had given careful consideration to what the women would enjoy singing. I had been so excited to finally teach whatever songs I wanted, without having to worry about the difficulty level for Ashkenazim. The room was too noisy, the organizers reasoned; it would be difficult to teach songs. Besides, they justified, there were women who might be offended by having to learn religious songs.

Offended by having to learn religious songs? It was the first time in my life I heard of hostility towards religious traditions coming from the Mizrahi/Sephardi community. For millennia, even as Mizrahi and Sephardi Jews followed a strictly religious path, they had lived with a balance between religious and secular life, functioning simultaneously in the worlds of business, law, medicine, government, and Judaism.

My own experience with Mizrahim and Sephardim always was a *misoratee* experience, where one could say Kiddush on *Shebbath* and then have the traditional meal, while playing cassette tapes of Mizrahi music. One could call family by telephone to wish them *Shebbath Shalom,* return to the *Shebbath* table to sing *Sh'bahoth,* and finish off the evening in the living room, watching Arabic television. During my visits to Ramat Gan, where my Jewish family had lived since around 1950, I had experiences of walking to synagogue while neighbors drove to the beach, honking and waving at us, *"Shabbat Shalom!"*

We went to the lounge area for our formal conference opening and open mic time. During the open mic, a seventy-year-old Iraqi Jewish woman named Louise got up and began reading in Judeo-Arabic about the oppression her parents had faced in Israel. "It is important to me to read this to you in Arabic," she said, "because I avoided the language for so long, as a part of my self-hatred of our culture. But it is a part of our heritage, and we all must learn it and use it."

Louise read. And read. The letter went on and on. People got restless, and the facilitators asked Louise to stop, saying the letter was too long and that she was being unfair to the women who did not understand it. Louise refused. "If people don't understand what I'm saying," she said, "let it stand as an indication of a problem—namely, why don't we understand the language of our tradition? If we don't understand it, we need to learn it." Louise continued, and people got angry.

I felt torn. I understood the facilitators' organizational concerns, but I thought what Louise was doing was important. She was reading about her parents' oppression, in her parents' native language, in the same or similar native language of all the Mizrahi women's parents and grandparents. She was making a wonderful point about our identity and what we had lost of it. I did not understand one single word of what she was saying, and I too thought the letter was too long; but I did not care. I wanted Louise to continue. I quieted people, trying to help her be heard.

The facilitators repeatedly asked Louise to stop, but Louise kept reading. There was a lot of commotion in the room, with people both strongly in favor of and against Louise continuing. Finally, the facilitators took the microphone away from Louise. "This is not about the letter," the facilitators said, "or about it being in Arabic. The letter is too long to stand and read here. It is not fair to everyone else. We need to give time for everyone and continue with our program." I believed the facilitators. I knew them, knew that they would be the last to be against Mizrahim learning and speaking Arabic. I understood their position. Still, I could not help but be delighted by Louise's insurrection.

Open mic ended, and we cleared all the chairs off the floor. Margalit Tsinani, a popular Mizrahi singer, was our guest performer. I was excited—I had a tape of hers, and I loved it.

She was one Mizrahi woman who filled her space. Watching her command the audience and her band, I was reminded of strong African-American women I had admired. She was a beautiful, large woman. She wore clothes that showed off her figure, and she looked fantastic. I wished there were more images of big, strong, beautiful women. She laughed loud, she said it like it was, and she was one of mine!

We all danced North African/Middle Eastern style, waving our arms around in the air. I always danced that way in night-clubs, but usually I was the only one doing it. Strangely, at the conference I felt pressure to dance this way and do it "right." I had a growing sense of alienation as "The American," making me feel I needed to prove my Mizrahi-ness to everyone.

I was dancing with a group of young women, including a Druze woman, Amal, with whom I felt a strong connection. She wore a traditional Arab dress and head cover.

Margalit introduced the next song and said that she did not go places, did not do shows, without bringing her politics with her. She said something about having learned that from her mother. The next song was about Jerusalem "which," she said, "is and must always remain united, as the capital of Israel." Many women cheered. Amal, however, looked at her friend and said, "I don't agree." She left the dance floor, and her friend followed. Once again, I felt torn. I kept dancing as the Jerusalem song began, but I felt saddened by Amal's departure.

On Saturday morning, I woke up early and went to breakfast. I sat at a table with a young Mizrahi woman and finally had a real conversation with another attendee. I was thrilled. We sat and talked for an hour, even as breakfast ended and people left. I felt that I had finally made a friend at the conference. We dis-cussed all kinds of issues about Mizrahi identity and then laughed, realizing both of us had originally thought the other was Ashkenazi because of our light skin.

At my first workshop, we addressed the questions, "What does it mean to be a young Mizrahi woman? How do we define ourselves?" An Ashkenazi reporter who was writing an article on the conference attended the workshop. She requested that women who wanted to speak with her in detail about this issue meet her afterwards. I volunteered myself. "But you're Anglo-Saxon," she said.

Anglo-Saxon? That was a first! I had spent most of my life feeling inferior for *not* being Anglo-Saxon. I had felt ugly because of my Mediterranean features, and I had felt ashamed for being a Jew. Suddenly at a Mizrahi feminist conference, I was called Anglo-Saxon and alienated for this mistaken identity. "No, I'm not!" I replied, dumbfounded. Other women chimed in, "She's Mizrahi!" The reporter apologized.

Each woman took turns expressing what encompassed our Mizrahi identity. At the end of the workshop, the reporter again asked women to gather around her if they wanted to be interviewed. I was the first to approach; I did not want to be late for the next workshop. Two other women followed. We went outside and sat on the lawn. I sat directly in front of the reporter, but she turned to face a woman on my left, who had arrived after me, and began asking questions. I was annoyed, but I said nothing. The interview took a long time, and I was anxious about being late for my next workshop. Finally, the reporter finished. *Oh, good,* I thought. But then she swiveled around to interview the woman on my right.

I was being ignored.

I could tell the reporter saw me as a less legitimate Mizrahi, because I was American. I was upset by how much I had been brushed off and ignored throughout the conference by then. "Excuse me," I said, "Can I ask you a question?"

"No," she said, putting up a hand and looking annoyed. "I'm busy now."

I walked away and began crying. *No,* I thought to myself, *this is not okay. I did not come this far to feel alienated. This is my conference too, and I am going to* make *it mine.* I turned around and went back.

"Excuse me," I said to the reporter. "I need to tell you something."

"Wait until I'm done," the reporter said, again barely looking at me. "I'm in the middle of interviewing."

"No," I said. "I won't wait. This is not okay. It seems you think I am less legitimate of a Mizrahi because I'm American."

"G-d forbid!" the reporter exclaimed. "I just didn't notice you."

Exactly my point.

"I didn't mean anything by it," she continued. "I'll interview you right after I finish with her." She looked back at the woman she was interviewing.

"No," I insisted. "I've been waiting, and you just skipped over me. This is not okay."

"But she has to get to her workshop," the reporter said of the interviewee.

"Well, so do I!" I replied, exasperated.

"Well, just wait," the reporter said.

I left, upset by what had happened but glad I had confronted the reporter. I had been inspired by the Mizrahi women around me: I knew none of them would have asked if they could ask a question. They just would have said what was on their mind and insisted that they be heard. Seeing them in action gave me that strength.

I went to my next workshop, "The Existence (or Erasure) of Mizrahi Identity in Education." As a Jewish multicultural educator, the workshop was just up my alley.

The facilitator posed a question to the group, asking about our experiences in education: What did we learn or not learn about Mizrahim? I listened as each woman recounted experiences of invisibility that paralleled my own. Finally I spoke up, sharing that my education about Jews only discussed Ashkenazim, and my education about North Africans and Middle Easterners only discussed Arabs. My identity was absent in both my Jewish and secular education, and growing up with hardly any other Mizrahim, I had no community to which to turn.

"But that's in America," the facilitator said. "This is different." She moved on with the workshop.

I went numb, and I did not hear another word for the next ten minutes. When I came back to consciousness, I desperately wanted to leave. My eyes burned from anger and holding back tears. *Stay,* I told myself. *Stay till the end, and speak up about what has happened.*

"*Ein homar . . . Ein homar . . .*" There is no material, the women kept saying. It was the same problem I faced in the United States. "When I do groundbreaking Mizrahi programs," a woman said, "the media presents them as side issues, as 'special interest' programs." It was the same problem I faced in the United States. I could have been having intense discussions with these women about the commonality of our Mizrahi struggle, no matter where we were in the world. I could have been sharing my own challenges and successes in overcoming our common obstacles.

Near the end, I raised my hand. "There is something really disturbing me," I said, "which I have to speak about. As I listened to all of you speak, I heard you discussing the exact experiences I have had. It doesn't matter where we are from. A Mizrahi is a Mizrahi. And regardless of where we live, we struggle against our invisibility. The difference between you and me is that you have each other here. I am almost alone where I live. I had to come across an ocean to finally be in a community of Mizrahi women. And here you are telling me once again that I am different, that I don't belong. If I don't belong here, where exactly do I belong?"

The facilitator sincerely apologized. A woman in the group thanked me "for speaking out instead of being silent about this. It showed us we have even more places to stretch. We need to look inside our community and address the issues within." I felt validated, and I also felt the American issue was finally over. I had said my piece, and I had gotten support.

After lunch, there was some free time. I had found out about a woman who filmed documentaries on Mizrahim, and I was interested in doing similar work, so I went over to speak with her. As I sat down next to her, another woman approached me, saying I should not have led Kiddush at dinner the night before, that it was not a Muswa, that it was a sin and disgrace, because a woman is not allowed to lead Kiddush. Arguing on a purely Halachic level, I countered that there was nothing in Jewish law against a woman leading this ritual. "There were men there," she replied. "It was very wrong of you to say Kiddush."

"She's right," the documentary woman chimed in.

I left, shaking inside. I soon ran into Louise, who remembered me from an Iraqi-Israeli conference ten years earlier, when I was sixteen. Either the designated song leader had been singing Ashkenazi songs, or he had done a poor job leading Mizrahi songs, I cannot remember. All I know is that at some point I had jumped on top of a table and started leading everyone in lively Iraqi songs, and I was a hit.

I could not focus on what Louise was saying. "Loolwa,

what's wrong with you?" she finally asked. I started to tell her, in a controlled voice, about what had just happened. The lump in my throat exploded, and I began to shake and sob. "Oh, *mumi*," she said lovingly. "Come here." She led me to a table and chairs, and we sat down. I cried and cried, telling her the story. Her sister Marselle joined us. They both were furious at what the woman had said about my leading Kiddush, and they told me what an idiot she was. "Show me who this woman is," Louise demanded. "I want to talk to her. I'll give her something to cry about! Just show me who she is."

Louise told me a woman had approached her the night before, saying she was not a Jew but an Arab, because she had insisted on reading in Arabic. "That's ridiculous!" I declared. "I can't believe she told you that!"

"You see?" Louise said. "People say stupid things. You can't listen to them." Louise and Marselle confirmed for me that from a Halachaic viewpoint, the woman was wrong about my not being allowed to lead Kiddush, and they listed all the rabbis I could ask for confirmation. Marselle made me laugh hard, and Louise was delighted to see me happy again.

It was wonderful to be supported by older Mizrahi women. My grandmother died before I was born, and although I have many Mizrahi aunts, I had no role models of strong Mizrahi women. I never could talk with my aunts about what I really thought, what I really experienced in the world. It was so nourishing to be around older Mizrahi women who spoke their minds and supported my visibility.

I left Louise and Marselle to attend my next workshop on Ethiopian women's identity struggle. Up to that point, my contact with Ethiopian Jews had been with individuals who neither identified as feminist nor acknowledged racism against the Ethiopian community. This workshop was run by women my age, and I felt energized to see other young women leading workshops about issues affecting women of all ages.

Shortly after I arrived, the workshop facilitators began discussing how they disliked being asked questions about their community's history, traditions, and struggles. I had looked forward to the workshop and to speaking with the facilitators one-on-one, as a way of gathering more information to include in my Jewish multicultural programming. If the facilitators did not want to be asked such questions, I wondered, how could I find out more about the Ethiopian Jewish community? When I raised my concern, the facilitators clarified that random strangers felt perfectly comfortable asking very personal questions. "In the context of friendship," one facilitator responded, "I am happy to answer these questions. My friends and I discuss very personal things."

"But people come up to me on a bus," the other facilitator continued "and ask me about my life in Ethiopia: what my immigration experience was like, what kinds of struggles I face here. Nobody would go up to a random Ashkenazi and begin asking such personal questions."

The facilitators went on to say that people need to do their homework, to take the time to find out about Ethiopian Jews. "What kind of material is available in Israel regarding the Ethiopian community?" I asked. "Is it written by Ethiopians? If not, is it written with consciousness and respect, or is it paternalistic, patronizing?"

"There's not a lot of information in Hebrew," one facilitator responded. "What does exist is not usually written by Ethiopians and is not that good."

In the States, whenever I went to presentations about Ethiopian Jews, I heard the refrain, "Ethiopian children are integrating well." I always snorted to myself, understanding the real meaning: "Ethiopian children are successfully being bleached of their heritage." Inevitably, the Americans running these presentations whipped out their little videotapes and confirmed my fears, showing images of Ethiopian children wearing Western clothing and singing Ashkenazi-Israeli songs. The people who celebrated these images made me want to bang my head against a wall. Why, I wondered, are people who care about the survival of Ethiopian Jews not equally concerned about the survival of Ethiopian Jewish heritage?

"When I came here," I shared with the Ethiopian facilitators later on in the workshop, "I thought of Mizrahim and Ethiopians as being all together, in the same boat. I felt a natural connection with Ethiopian Jews, like with Mizrahi Jews. Do you feel a natural connection and alliance with Mizrahim?"

"We are *not* Mizrahim," one facilitator responded emphatically. "People keep trying to clump us together with Mizrahim, but we are our own community. We are different than Mizrahim. Yes, we have points of alliance. Yes, we have similar struggles. It is true that Ashkenazim are above all of us [in the socio-political hierarchy]. Ashkenazim are here." She gestured with her hand above her head. "And Mizrahim are here." She gestured far below where she had indicated the rank of Ashkenazim. "But we are here." She moved her hand one step below the Mizrahim.

It was the first time I had heard of this reality, and my "family" visions shattered. For me, having grown up invisible in the Ashkenazi reality of American Judaism, and having fought this invisibility all my life, I felt kindred to all non-Ashkenazi Jews: Whether Jews were of Indian, Ethiopian, Turkish, Yemenite, or Mexican heritage, I felt we were one in our struggle to be heard, in our fight to save our culture before it disappeared before our very eyes. In the United States, people from these non-Ashkenazi communities seem to feel the same. But in this workshop, I sadly discovered that in Israel, there are divisions and strife between Ethiopian Jews and Mizrahim/Sephardim.

I was unsure whether the facilitators would feel enough of a connection with me to start a relationship, having heard their experience of Mizrahim as part ally and part oppressor. After the workshop, I caught up with the facilitators outside. I shared my confusion about how exactly to approach them, if at all. We did exchange phone numbers, but it felt awkward, not the scenario I had imagined before the conference.

Soon it was time for closing mic, and I got in line to speak. Amal was before me. "Yesterday," she said to the group, "I felt so comfortable with everyone. I felt a part of everything, and I danced with everyone as if we were sisters. I felt more comfortable dancing here than I would in my own village. At one point, Margalit began singing the song about Jerusalem, and she said Jerusalem should be the united capital under Israel. I suddenly felt alienated from everyone." Amal stated that Margalit should not have said those words.

Women clapped. Women booed. Women shouted angrily. Women argued with each other. Amal paused, smiled, and stood looking out at the chaos. She seemed so centered and strong.

I disagreed with Amal. I felt that Mizrahi women had to

have the conference space to explore and express our own identity, and I happened to agree with Margalit's statement about Jerusalem. But I admired Amal for standing there and saying what she believed, when it clearly was not popular.

After people calmed down, it was Louise's turn to speak. "Last night, a woman came over to me and told me I am not a Jew but an Arab," Louise recounted, "because I read my letter in Arabic. Arabic is part of our heritage, and we need to learn it. Yesterday, I was not allowed to finish reading my letter. I am going to finish it now."

Louise started reading her letter from where she had left off the night before. The facilitators let her read for a while, then tried to stop her. People shouted at her and at each other. At one point, when it was too loud for anyone to hear her, she stopped, looked up at the pandemonium, and smiled. She then turned to face me and shook her butt in a little dance. I burst into laughter.

Finally, the facilitators took the mic from her, again explaining to everyone their position on the matter. They then handed the mic to me, but the pandemonium continued. I handed the mic back to a facilitator, who hushed the crowd. As it began to quiet, a woman in the crowd shouted, "Oh, and are you going to speak in English now?" Women laughed in response. I saw the humor, but I also was annoyed. I had crammed two Hebrew classes and daily vocabulary practice before leaving home, and I had struggled all conference long to speak only Hebrew. I ignored the comment and began to talk.

I expressed how important the conference was to me. I shared that it was hard in various ways and that I had cried many times, but that of course it would be hard the first time we came together to discuss our identity. I reminded everyone that Mizrahi women are all over the world now, and that we have to recognize and honor the Mizrahi struggle, no matter where it is.

I told them about the woman who said I had sinned by leading *kiddush*. "We need to create Mizrahi women's prayer space," I asserted, "where women are leading the prayers for ourselves and others. We need to figure out how to claim our religious traditions for ourselves as women, instead of just accepting them as is or leaving them altogether. Religious traditions are a fundamental part of Mizrahi culture. The secular/religious split comes from Ashkenazi Zionist influence. It is not ours."

More women followed. A woman I had not met began to speak. Because of the speed and vocabulary with which she spoke, it was difficult for me to follow all her Hebrew, but I got this much: "As Mizrahim, we share a lot with Arabs. We have common music, language, food. I live in an area with many Arabs. But this conference is Mizrahi space. And I'll be damned if we can't talk about our identity in our own space. I am an Israeli woman, and Jerusalem is Israel's capital, and that is part of my identity."

All hell broke loose. Women cheered, women shouted angrily, and women stormed out of the room. The speaker continued, but I could not hear her above all the chaos.

A big contingent of women clapped, and I agreed with them silently. With the backdrop of Mizrahi women being loud and proud about their politics, it became clear how quiet I was, how quiet I had been for years. I was used to my politics being subsumed by Eurocentric constructs, definitions, and judgments, used to my Mizrahi background being completely invisible. I had learned to shut up, knowing nobody would understand me or my reasons for my politics.

In the past, whenever I had voiced my feelings about Arab-Jewish/Arab-Israel relations, people had jumped down my throat, reciting to me the Palestinian cause—as if it could not exist side-by-side with the Mizrahi cause, as if there were room for only one, as if the pain of Person A's broken arm meant Person B could not share the pain of her broken leg. Repeatedly I had been forced into two opposing camps: Either I was progressive/pro-Arab/pro-Palestinian and thus in favor of giving up the West Bank, Gaza, East Jerusalem, and the Golan Heights, or I was racist/anti-Arab/anti-Palestinian and in favor of keeping all or part of the land.

In all the analyses I had heard, from the Left and the Right, the so-called doves and hawks, there had been a poignant lack of awareness of Mizrahi reality—as if the only refugees were Arab, the only Jews were European, and "Jewish" and "Middle Eastern" identities were diametrically opposed.

I felt that Arabs and Jews needed to talk about all the Arab-Jewish/Arab-Israeli points of connection and oppression, and only then begin thinking of how to solve the problems in the Middle East. Without looking at the full picture, I felt, there was a lack of integrity in addressing Arab-Israel relations.

Reflecting on the reasons for my silence in the past, I looked at the women clapping. "It is finally safe here," I said to myself. "My identity is not split here. There is an understanding here." I clapped. I was still uncomfortable, but it felt good.

Amal passed me, storming out. I felt as if I were hiding something, then felt guilty, then angry that I felt guilty. Did Amal feel guilty for what she had said? Did she worry whether she was hurting me by storming out after a Mizrahi woman claimed the right to her own voice and space?

I held the perspective that Mizrahim are an indigenous people fighting for their right to their own piece of land in their own region, without being hassled or subsumed by Arab Muslim rule anymore. I saw us as being engaged in a struggle to have the collective room to breathe.

Throughout North Africa and the Middle East, Jews were *dhimmis*—second-class, inferior people. Islam and Muslims were made to be, literally and figuratively, always above Judaism and Jews. Even in the mildest forms of discrimination, Jews were treated as subordinate. This dynamic meant that Jews could participate in the society around them, enjoy a certain degree of wealth and status, and befriend their Arab Muslim neighbors, but they always had to know their "place." It is with this information, understanding, and personal experience that many Mizrahim approach and have insight into the issue of Arab-Israel relations.

With rare exceptions, I had not experienced Arab willingness to make room for this perspective on Arab-Jewish/Arab-Israel issues; rather, I felt pressure that to be friends or allies, I first had to deny my own reality. As such, to be connected, I felt I had to endanger myself, participate in diminishing my own space. With Amal storming out, I felt this issue rise to the surface again.

"People," one of the facilitators said, "we want to hear everything you have to say. That is why we have the open mic. Please use it instead of shouting. We can't communicate if everyone is yelling." The facilitators kept trying to bring order to the room, but the emotions ran too high to be controlled.

One of the Druze women storming out turned around and shouted in a booming voice. "You play *our* music, you speak *our* language, you eat *our* food, you take *our* culture. But you don't care about that, do you?"

In college, I founded a group to educate students about Mizrahim and Sephardim, and the group's first program was learning North African and Middle Eastern songs for Rosh Hashanah. When I called the Arab Student Association to discuss cosponsoring the program, the representative was hostile, saying, "This is another example of Jews taking over what is Arab. You take Jewish songs and put them to Arab tunes, you take Arab food and call it Israeli."

Since when do Arabs own everything North African and Middle Eastern? I thought in response. The Jewish people are indigenous to the Middle East and North Africa, having lived in the region since time immemorial. Judaism, furthermore, predates Islam by over 2,500 years and any Arab presence in much of the region by over 1,000 years. *So who exactly is taking what from whom?*

Ultimately, I found it absurd to get into such pettiness. The fact is that many different tribes lived together in North Africa and the Middle East for thousands of years. It is impossible and, furthermore, irrelevant to determine who made up what and who "took it" from whom. We all created a culture together, and it belongs to all of us equally. Trying to assert that one group has more legitimacy and entitlement than another is inherently being hateful toward one's neighbors. Furthermore, it is being hateful toward oneself, as it is denying neighboring threads which are part of the fabric of one's own heritage.

Louise called to everyone as she re-entered the room and said, "There are five Druze women upstairs, and they are crying their eyes out. I think we should go upstairs and be with them." Women left and followed her. I was touched by Louise's care and call to action. Enough women responded to the call that I did not feel I needed to go. I wanted to comfort these women and did not want them to hurt. Based on past experiences, however, I felt they would not accept my gesture of friendship because of my politics, and I did not want to feel rejected.

The facilitators managed to calm the remaining women down enough to proceed with the open mic. Two women stood up to speak about the commotion and their feelings about what Margalit had said. Between speakers, one of the facilitators asked people to remember the rest of the conference as well: "We're letting the statement of one person disrupt the whole conference. There is so much more to discuss. We do not agree with Margalit's comments about Jerusalem. They were racist. Jews had a good life in Arab countries." A few women hissed loudly. "They didn't put Jews in gas chambers," the facilitators said in response.

"Yes, but they tried!" I called out, surprised to hear my own voice audibly.

What exactly is our point of reference for determining "a good life?" I wondered. Do we hold over our heads Europe's extermination of six million Jews and gratefully accept anything less? How about characterizing a "good life" as living in a place where we can hold our heads up high, be loud and proud about who we are, have autonomy, and take up space without fear?

I reflected on the words of a friend, a young Iranian woman who had told me that Jews had a great life in Iran, problem-free. Just a few sentences later, however, she revealed that her parents had left the country because they were afraid. "Well, why were they afraid?" I had pressed, curious about the contradictory statements. "Oh, you know," she had answered, "stuff like how when they were growing up, Muslims threw stones at them and other Jewish children going to school."

The inability to see our own oppression, I mused, comes

from having lived victim to it for so long. Saying that Jews had a "good life" in Arab countries is similar to saying that a woman is "lucky" if her husband slaps her around or constantly puts her down, but does not brutally beat or kill her.

As the open mic continued, the women who had stormed out came back in. One of the Druze women took the mic and said, "I felt very angry that Louise was not allowed to finish reading the letter read in Arabic. I spent the entire conference struggling to understand everything in Hebrew, and you couldn't tolerate a few minutes of listening to Arabic? Hearing the letter was the only time I could really understand what was going on."

Two other women took the mic. They were close friends, one Mizrahi and one Palestinian. They spoke about how they loved and supported each other. They gave hope that we all can coexist. The mood began to change, and the storm seemed to be over. I was inspired seeing women feeling their anger passionately, expressing it, acting on it, and then moving past it—a turbulent yet necessary process.

The facilitators thanked the women for returning and began to say closing words. I was scheduled to lead a *Shebbath* song for the closing ceremony, but one of the facilitators approached me and asked which song I planned to sing. When I told her, she asked me to pick another one. "Why?" I asked.

"Because it mentions Jerusalem. Pick something that doesn't mention Jerusalem. To be politically correct, you know." I scanned the text of my chosen song.

"But it doesn't mention Jerusalem."

"Okay," she said, "then it's fine."

I felt agitated. Singing about Jerusalem is a fundamental part of being a Jew. Longing to return to our homeland is at the core of all Jewish prayer, as it has been for thousands of years.

This yearning is repeated over and over again in our daily, Sabbath, and holiday prayers, our after-meal blessings, our songs.

Not one day in my life was I not aware of Jerusalem, did I not know where it was in relation to where I was standing. Every single day, healthy or sick, at home or traveling, I woke up, figured out the direction to Jerusalem, and faced it, reciting *Modeh Ani,* the prayer thanking G-d for being alive—just as my ancestors had done every morning for 2,600 years. Every time I blessed bread before a meal, I dipped it in salt to remember the destruction of the Holy Temple in Jerusalem—just as my ancestors had done every time before eating, for 2,600 years.

I found and still find it unacceptable to insist I erase or hide my reality in deference to someone else's reality. It is undeniable that there is a clash over claims to Jerusalem. What Jews, Arabs, and the rest of the world ultimately decide to do with this struggle can be negotiated. What I find nonnegotiable is the reality of the various identities and histories of the people involved.

Mizrahi history must be honored as legitimate. Our songs and prayers, the voice of our ancestors, must be honored as an inseparable part of who we are. If the fallout of inviting Arab women to the conference was silencing the Mizrahi voice, then I feel it was premature to invite the Arab women to come.

When I finally was allowed to sing, people clapped and sang along. When I finished, a crowd of women gathered around me, praising me. "I'm crazy about this person!" one of the women exclaimed. Mizrahi music began to play from one of the speakers, and women began dancing. Eventually, most of the women left. Amal and I, however, continued dancing with each other.

Amal's cousin came to pick her up, bringing an Arabic CD

featuring an Arab singer. "Oh, good," Amal said, "now we can listen to the *real thing.*" Amal handed me the CD and instructed me to have the bartender put it on, instead of the music playing. She spoke to me conspiratorially, as if we were in something together, bonding over her definition of Middle Eastern-ness.

The music playing was a very popular Mizrahi-Israeli song. It *was* the real thing to me—about my community and in my people's language. I felt that to call the Arab CD "the real thing," as opposed to the Mizrahi music, was to subtly further Arab claims on North African and Middle Eastern culture. Amal not only put forth Arab music as more legitimate than Mizrahi music, but to add insult to injury, she wanted me to be the one to silence the Mizrahi song and replace it with the Arab one.

The interaction was symbolic of the ways I have felt obliterated by other people's constructs of who I am. It was a strange yet telling ending to the first conference for Mizrahi women. It showed how very far we have yet to go.

ENDNOTES

Vashti

1. (Tanakh, 1985, p.1457)
2. Ibid, 1458
3. Ibid
4. (Meador, 1994, p.216)
5. Tanakh, 1459
6. Ibid
7. Ibid, 1462–3

Breaking the Silence

1. This piece is a translated transcript of three speeches delivered by Mizrahi women at the plenary session of the Tenth National Feminist Conference in Israel, July 17–19, 1994. The following introduction to the speeches paraphrases excerpts from the introduction of *News From Within*'s editor Tikva Honig-Parnass.

Ashkenazi Eyes

1. *Chah'Chahim* is a pejorative term for working-class Mizrahim, implying stereotypes such as pushy, loud, overly sexual, and swindling.

2. I use the term "Israeli-Palestinian" to describe people usually referred to as "Israeli-Arabs," both because these individuals frequently identify as Palestinians with Israeli citizenship and because I see the term "Arab" as encompassing Christians, Muslims, and Jews.

3. My Mizrahi adaptation of Emma Goldman's "If I can't dance, it's not my revolution." Iraqi Jews hold henna parties on the night before the wedding, to wish good fortune upon the bride.

Reflections of an Arab Jew
(notes added by editor)

1. World-renowned Egyptian rabbi, physician, and philosopher; born in Spain (1135–1204)

2. By traditional Jewish law, women have to cover their heads after marrying. In Ashkenazi practice, women traditionally wear wigs to cover their hair. In more orthodox Ashkenazi circles, women shave their heads, wear wigs over their shaved heads, and wear hats on top.

3. *Al Neharoth Babel* is a traditional Jewish prayer that says, "By the rivers of Babylon we sat and wept, when we remembered Zion." Jews wrote this prayer in expression of their grief about being exiled to Babylon from ancient Israel.

In Exile at Home

1. *"Defiled"* was chosen by the translator as the most suitable interpretation for *najjes shodan,* a Muslim-Iranian colloquialism referring to the polluting of objects by the hands of dogs, pigs, Jews, etc. In the present context, the particular religious connotation of *najjes shodan* also reflects the then general belief in Khomeini's holiness.

2. *"sister"* here has explicit revolutionary connotations, much like "comrade" would in a Bolshevik context.

Illusion in Assimilation

1. Phurer, Ruth, "The Image of the Mizrahi Edot." *Iyyunim be Khinuch* #45, 1986.

2. Shmueli, A., *Toldot Amenu Ba Zman Ha Chadash* Vol. 7, (Tel Aviv: Yavne) 1970.

3. ibid., p. 414

4. Kipnis, L., *Rumiah the Little Nanny* (Tel Aviv: Lichtenfeld), 1981.

5. Fuerstein, K. and Rochel M., *The Children of the Melah—The Cultural Retardation Among Moroccan Children and its Meaning in Education.* Jewish Agency, 1953.

6. Frankenstein, K., "On Ethnic Difference." *Megamot* Vol. B3, 1951.

7. Frankenstein, K., "On the Concept of Primitivity." *Megamot* Vol. B3, 1951.

8. Simon, A. E., "On the Meaning of the Concept of Primitivity." *Megamot* Vol. B3, 1951.

9. Rottenstreich, N., "An Absolute Measurement" *Megamot* volume B3, 1951.

10. Eisenstadt, S. N., *Immigration Absorption.* Hebrew University, 1951.

11. Eisenstadt, S. N., *Israel: A Society in the Making.* Akademon, 1967.

12. ibid.

13. Eisenstadt, S. N., "Leadership. Problems Among the 'Olim,'" *Megamot* Vol. D2, 1953.

14. ibid.

15. Rabinian, D., "Nuvo Frenkit," *Hadashot*, Section Ha'Ir, 29 September 1993.

16. A semiformal national hymn.

How the Camel Found Its Wings
1. *Ha-gamal Ha-me'ofef.* Dir. Rami Na'aman, 1994.
2. George Lenczowski, *The Middle East in World Affairs,* fourth edition. (Ithaca: Cornell University Press, 1987), 415.

We Are Here and This Is Ours
1. Hebrew is a Semitic language, originating in North Africa and the Middle East. Originally, Hebrew had a different pronunciation for each letter. The linguistic distinctions were preserved by the Mizrahi community, as this community stayed for thousands of years in the lands where such sounds are common to all languages. The Ashkenazi community, however, lost many of the distinctions after settling in Europe. Slavic and Germanic sounds are not compatible with many of the original pronunciations in Hebrew. As such, distinctions such as those between "h" and "ch," "w" and "v" were lost. Today, "standard" Hebrew taught in schools throughout the world follow a modified version of Ashkenazi Hebrew, where many letters do not bear distinctions. Though the Mizrahi accent preserves the pronunciations of original Hebrew, it is the subject of frequent ridicule in Jewish communities throughout the world.

GLOSSARY

aliyah: Literally means "ascent," referring to Jewish immigration to Israel.

Amharic: Ethiopian language.

Ashkenazi: Central/Eastern European Jewish.

ba'aba: White flour pastry filled with fried dates, and covered in sesame seeds.

band andaz: Depilator.

band andazi: Depilation.

bar mitzvah/bar muswa: A ritual celebration of a boy turning thirteen, when by Jewish law he becomes a man.

bat mitzah/bath muswa: A ritual celebration of a girl turning twelve, when by Jewish law she becomes a woman.

bracha: Hebrew word for blessing.

brit/brith milah: A ritual circumcision of an eight-day-old baby boy.

bubbe: Yiddish for grandmother.

chador: Fullbody veil worn by Iranian women.

chiturini: Chicken curry, a traditional Indian dish.

Converso: A Jew converted to Christianity as part of the mass forced conversion in Spain and Portugal in the Middle Ages. *Conversos* usually remained Jews in secret.

couscous: Morocco's national dish, made of semolina wheat.

dhimmi: Jews and Christians under Islam—"people of The Book"—were given the status of a tolerated yet inferior people, severely restricted in terms of movement, dress, economic opportunity and social standing.

djellabah: A long, loose-fitting hooded robe or gown worn by men in Morocco.

dowry: The gift that a bride's family gives to the couple, but in essence, it goes to the groom's family.

Druze: A small religious community, with members in Syria, Lebanon, and Israel. Druze speak Arabic and follow a social pattern very similar to the Arabs of the region but traditionally consider themselves neither Arabs nor Muslims. Some 300,000 Druze live in the Middle East today. The religion developed out of Ismaili Islam, a religio-political movement based in the Fatimid Caliphate, in the tenth century.

Farhud: The pro-Nazi torture and massacre of Jews and pillaging of Jewish property in 1941 in Iraq.

ghalyoun: A water pipe, or hookah.

Gut Shabbes: Yiddish for "peaceful Sabbath."

Halacha: Jewish law, according to the Talmud.

Halachic: Of or related to the Halacha, Jewish law.

hamsa: The Middle Eastern symbol for the hand of G-d, also known as a shadai in the Jewish communities.

Hassidic/Chassidic: Following an eighteenth-century Eastern European Jewish movement that became a sect of Judaism and that emphasized the spirit of Jewish law over the word of the law. The Hassidic movement currently is affiliated with the ultra-Orthodox stream of Judaism.

henna: The dye used on skin and hair, in ceremonies such as weddings, throughout North Africa and the Middle East and certain areas of the Far East.

Insh'allah: G-d willing.

Judeo: Jewish.

Judeo-Arabic: The language spoken by Jews throughout North Africa and the Middle East. It is a blend of Hebrew and the Arabic dialect of a particular region.

juive: French for a Jew.

ka'ak: A cardamom flavored white-flour pastry.

kabbalistic: From the Kabbalah, the Jewish mystical text.

Kaddish: The Jewish mourning prayer.

kashered: Made kosher.

kashrut: The laws and system of keeping kosher.

Khanoum: A title equivalent to Mrs. or Miss, used after a

woman's name, reflecting formal speech toward women, comparable to Southern speech in the United States.

kibbutz: A farm- or other land-based settlement established throughout Israel, which adheres to the traditional Communist model of shared property for all members.

kibbutzim: Plural of kibbutz.

kibbutznik: Someone who grew up on a kibbutz. *Kibbutzniks* are usually Ashkenazi and secular.

Kiddush: The Hebrew word for the ritual prayer said during the Jewish Sabbath and holy days, blessing wine, bread, and fruits from the tree and the earth.

Kief: Moroccan marijuana, a mixture of grass and tobacco usually smoked in a pipe.

Kol Nidre: A prayer said on Yom Kippur absolving Jews of all oaths made under force. The prayer was developed in response to the forced conversions of Jews throughout the world.

kosher: Following the religious dietary laws of Judaism, including rules for what animals are permissible to kill for consumption, what methods of killing are permissible, how meat must be cooked and what can and cannot be eaten with meat.

mehisa/mechitza: A four-foot wall, minimum, separating men and women in synagogues. In ultra-Orthodox communities, the wall may reach from floor to ceiling. Traditionally, women in Mizrahi and Sephardi communities were a floor above the men, where they observed unobstructed from balconies. In the United States, the *mehisa* is most often positioned with the men in front and the women in back; more progressive congregations have the wall down the center of the synagogue, with women and men on separate sides.

mehrieh: Money owed the bride in case of divorce.

mellah: Jewish ghetto in Morocco.

Minha: Jews traditionally pray three times a day—morning, afternoon, and night. *Minha* is the afternoon prayer.

Mishna: Jewish tradition teaches that this collection of oral Jewish laws was received alongside the Torah (the written Bible) on Mount Sinai. It was passed on from generation to generation until Rabbi Yehuda Hanassi wrote and edited it in a book, so it would not be forgotten. According to Jewish tradition, one cannot be understood properly without the other.

Misoratee: Traditional religious but not Orthodox.

mitzvah/muswa: A good deed required by Jewish law.

mitzvot/muswoth: Plural of *mitzvah/muswa.*

Mizrahi: Literally meaning "Eastern" in Hebrew, it refers to Jewish communities indigenous to North Africa and the Middle East, as well as Jewish communities from Central and East Asia.

Moshav: A community living on the same land, with each family owning its own property.

Neilah: The closing service for Yom Kippur.

noghl: A candy made of flour, sugar, rose water, and almonds.

nusah: Hebrew word for tradition or style, specifically referring to Mizrahi, Sephardi, Ethiopian, or Ashkenazi Jewish customs.

Pesah: Passover, the Jewish holiday celebrating the Jews' exodus from Egypt.

Pieds Noirs: Literally meaning "black feet," this is the name given to the French born in Algeria, and it is used as a derogatory term for Jews and Arabs from North Africa.

Purim: The holiday celebrating the Jewish liberation in ancient Persia, following a plot by Haman, an advisor to King Ahasuerus, to annihilate all Jews in the empire.

Qadous: The Judeo-Arabic word for the ritual prayer said during the Jewish Sabbath and holy days—blessing wine, bread and fruits from the trees and the earth.

sabra: Literally meaning "cactus," this word is used to refer to Israeli-born Jews.

sambousak: A white-flour pastry. Various fillings include feta cheese and eggs, fried chickpeas, meat, and sugar, cardamom, rosewater, and walnuts.

Seder: Passover tradition of the ritual storytelling of the exodus from Egypt. It involves chanting passages, reenacting scenes from Exodus, and eating special foods.

Sephardi: Descending from the Jewish community of *Sepharad* (Spain) and Portugal.

S'fardic: Sephardi.

Shabbat/Shebbath: The Jewish Sabbath, which begins on Friday night at sundown and ends Saturday night at sunset. *Shebbath* is the Iraqi term.

Shabbat Shalom/Shebbath Shalom: Hebrew for "peaceful Sabbath."

Shabbes: Yiddish word for the Jewish Sabbath.

sharbat: A drink made of the essence of various fruits. The most common forms are sour cherry *sharbat* and quince *sharbat.*

Sh'bahoth: Religious songs for the Sabbath and holy days.

sheidel: A wig worn by married women in Ashkenazi Orthodox communities.

Shohed: An animal slaughterer who has undergone the requisite studies in Jewish law and ethics.

shtetl: A Jewish ghetto in Eastern Europe.

souk: An outdoor market, where people bargain on prices.

sukkah: An outdoor hut commemorating *Sukkot/Sukkoth.*

Sukkot/Sukkoth: A holiday commemorating the forty-year period that the people of Israel wandered through the Sinai Desert after leaving Egypt. During *Sukkot,* Jews traditionally build an outdoor hut, *sukkah,* and sleep in it for one week, the duration of the holiday.

tallit: Prayer shawl.

Talmud: The book combining the Mishnah and the Gemarah (commentary, interpretation, and discussion about the Mishnah).

Tefilin: Phylacteries, consisting of two boxes with parchment on which four Torah passages are written. Men tie *tefilin* on their arm and forehead each day during morning prayers.

Tehilim: Jewish psalms.

Torah: The Hebrew Bible.

yarmulkes: Yiddish for skull caps. Yarmulkes are worn by Jewish men to symbolize that they are always in the service of G-d.

Yehud: Arabic for Jew.

Yiddishkeit: Commonly used to mean the sum total of Jewish heritage, though it specifically refers to Central and Eastern European Jewish heritage. *Yiddishkeit* is derived from the word "Yiddish."

Yom Kippur: The Day of Atonement, during which Jews fast for twenty-five hours and pray all night and day, asking forgiveness for transgressions during the previous year.

ADDITIONAL BOOKS

Additional Books by Women of North African and Middle Eastern Jewish Heritage:

Joelle Bahloul. *The Architecture of Memory: A Jewish-Muslim Household in Colonial Algeria 1937–1962.* Cambridge University Press, 1996.

Marina Benjamin. *My Tongue Is Her Heart.* Dunow & Carlson, 2004.

Farideh Goldin. *Wedding Song: Memories of an Iranian Jewish Woman.* Brandeis University Press, 2003.

Carmit Delman. *Burnt Bread and Chutney: Growing up Between Cultures—A Memoir of an Indian Jewish Girl.* New York: Ballantine Books, 2002.

Gina Nahai. *Moonlight on the Avenue of Faith.* Washington Square Press, 2000.

Dorit Rabinyan. *Persian Brides.* George Braziller Inc., 1995.

Homa Sarshar. *In the Back Alleys of Exile.* Ketab Corporation, 1993.

Ruth Knafo Setton. *The Road to Fez.* Counterpoint Press, 2001.

Ella Shohat. *Israeli Cinema: East/West and the Politics of Representation.* University of Texas Press, 1989.

Bat Ye'or. *The Dhimmi: Jews and Christians Under Islam.* Associated University Press, Cranbury, NJ, 1985.

About the Contributors

Yael Arami is an activist whose work addresses the complex intersection of religious, social, political, and economic issues for Mizrahi women, and her articles on these topics have been featured in Israeli periodicals including *Noga* and *Kivun Mizrah*. She is co-founder of an egalitarian Mizrahi prayer group in Jerusalem, and she is a former board member of Ahoti (My Sister)—an organization focusing on the rights and economic advancement of working-class Mizrahi women in Israel. Yael is in her third year of studies at the Eastern Music Center, where she learns religious Mizrahi music and classical Eastern music. She has also received formal training in rabbinic studies, and her dream is to establish a progressive Mizrahi synagogue in Israel.

Gina Bublil Waldman is co-founder of Jews Indigenous to the Middle East and North Africa (JIMENA), through which she lectures widely about the history of Mizrahim and the Arab-Israel conflict. Prior to her work with JIMENA, Waldman worked extensively with Muslim refugees from Bosnia, for which she received the Martin Luther King, Jr. Humanitarian Award. In addition, she spent well over a decade as a leading activist in the Soviet Jewry movement.

Henriette Dahan Kalev is the head of the Gender Studies Program at the University of Ben-Gurion in the Negev, and she has a Ph.D. in political science. She has written many articles on Mizrahi feminism and general political culture in Israel. Together with other Mizrahi friends, she founded the Hakeshet Hademocratit HaMizrahit (The Democratic Mizrahi Movement) and Ahoti (My Sister)—an organization focusing on the rights and economic advancement of workingp-class Mizrahi women in Israel. Henriette is an activist on numerous other human rights issues as well.

Farideh Dayanim Goldin is the author of *Wedding Song: Memories of an Iranian-Jewish Woman* (Brandeis University Press, 2003) under the name Farideh Goldin, and her book is the first autobiography written in English by an Iranian Jew. She has published articles in anthologies and magazines including *To Mend the World: Women Reflect on 9/11, Turnings, Bridges,* and *Nashim.* Farideh studied math and English literature at Pahlavi University in Shiraz, Iran. She transferred to Old Dominion University in Virginia, where she received her B.A. in English Literature, M.A. in Humanities, graduate certificate in Women's Studies, and M.F.A. in creative writing.

Mira Eliezer is a third-year student at Michlala Academait Law School in Ramat Gan. She is co-founder of Tiduá, an alternative community college which she established with Mizrahi peers, and for ten years, she served as Assistant Director of HILA (Association for Education in the Poor Neighborhoods and Development Towns), offering counseling and support to parents challenging educational institutions. Mira also served as the manager of Hakeshet

Hademocratit Hamizrahit (The Democratic Mizrahi Movement), the office manager of the Tel Aviv branch of The Feminist Movement in Israel, and a volunteer for the Tel Aviv rape crisis center. She currently works as manager of the foreign affairs department at a local corporation.

Julie Iny is the associate director of Kids First, a multiracial organization of youth and adults working to transform the systems that serve youth in Oakland, California—including schools, city, and county government—through youth organizing, advocacy, and coalition building. Julie completed her undergraduate studies in ethnicity and public policy at the University of California at Berkeley. During this time, she cofounded A Jewish Voice for Peace—a grassroots organization in the San Francisco Bay Area, promoting coexistence and a just peace for the Israeli and Palestinian peoples. Julie credits the generosity and warmth of her Iraqi-Indian extended family, as well as the legacy of American Jewish involvement with labor, civil rights, and feminist struggles as sources of inspiration for her activism.

Ruth Knafo Setton is the author of the *The Road to Fez* (Counterpoint Press, 2001). The recipient of literary fellowships from the National Endowment of the Arts, Pennsylvania Council on the Arts, and PEN, among others, her fiction, poetry and creative nonfiction have appeared in many journals and anthologies, including *Best Contemporary Jewish Writing, The North American Review, Tikkun, Lilith, Another Chicago Magazine, The Jewish Quarterly,* and *Sephardic-American Voices.* Ruth has taught creative writing in the M.F.A. program at Georgia College & State University, and is now

Writer-in-Residence for the Berman Center for Jewish Studies at Lehigh University. She is the fiction editor of *Arts & Letters: A Journal of Contemporary Culture,* and she is working on a new novel and collection of poems.

Lital Levy is a doctoral candidate in the department of comparative literature at the University of California at Berkeley, where she works on modern Hebrew and Arabic literature and film, and she has furthered her graduate studies in Jerusalem and Cairo. A specialist in Mizrahi, Arab-Jewish, and Israeli/Palestinian topics, Lital is preparing her dissertation on the late nineteenth–early twentieth-century writing of Egyptian and Iraqi Jews. Her writing has appeared in publications including *Bridges, The Arab Studies Journal, Critical Sense,* the *Christian Science Monitor,* and *Jewish Film: A Resource Guide.*

Tikva Levy is the director of HILA (Association for Education in the Poor Neighborhoods and Development Towns), and her articles and poems have appeared in *News From Within* and *Keys to the Garden: New Israeli Writing* (San Francisco City Lights Books, 1996). She lives in Israel with her young daughter, Yasmin.

Bahareh Mobasseri Rinsler is a psychotherapist in private practice in Los Angeles, where she works with adults, children, and families. She received her B.A. in women's studies from UCLA, where she was co-founder of the first *Rosh Hodesh* Jewish women's ritual group, and she continued her graduate studies in clinical psychology at Antioch University. She lives with her husband, Gregg, and their dog, Papaya.

Mojgan Moghadam-Rahbar is a freelance writer and trans-lator of Iranian and American media, producer and host of *Radio Voice of Iran,* and the former editor-in-chief of *Peyman* magazine for young Iranian Jews in Los Angeles. She is the mother of two children and expecting a new baby.

Homa Sarshar is the founder of the Center for Iranian Jewish Oral History, as well as the author of two and editor of twelve books. Her latest single-author book, *Shaban Jafari,* was the number-one bestseller in several countries, including Iran, in 2003. From 1968 to 1978, Homa was a correspondent reporter, special events reporter, and columnist for *Zan-e ruz* weekly magazine and *Keyhan* daily newspaper in Iran, where she also worked as the television producer, director, and talk-show host of National Iranian Radio & Television. Homa has received numerous awards for her work, including the Medal for Special Achievement in Women's Rights, given by the Iranian Women's Organization of Tehran, Iran. She currently works with *Jaam-E-Jam* Television in the Los Angeles area, and *Yaran* Radio, broadcast globally via satellite.

Ella Shohat is a professor of cultural studies in the departments of art & public policy, Middle Eastern studies, and comparative literature at New York University. She has lectured and pub-lished extensively on the intersection of post-colonialism, mul-ticulturalism, and gender, both nationally and internationally. Her award-winning work includes the books *Israeli Cinema: East/West and the Politics of Representation* (University of Texas Press, 1989) and *Unthinking Eurocentrism* (co-authored with R. Stam, Routledge, 1994). Ella has curated a number of cul-tural events and has served on the editorial boards of several journals, including *Social Text, Critique, Jouvert,* and *Public Culture.* Her writings have been translated into numerous languages, including French, Spanish, Portuguese, Arabic, Hebrew, German, and Turkish.

Caroline (pronounced Carolene) **Smadja** is an author currently living in France and writing a short story collection. Her writing, which has been published in the United States, Canada, South Africa, and France, includes "Motherland," *(Kinesis,* April 2000), "After Dark" *(Jewish Affairs,* Fall 2001), "Healing" *(Upstairs at Duroc),* and "In Absentia" *(California Quarterly).* When Caroline is not writing, she teaches French and English to expatriates and works as an intercultural trainer. In addition, she is an active member of the Société d'Histoire des Juifs de Tunisie (Organization on the History of Jews from Tunisia).

Rachel Wahba has a private psychotherapy practice in the San Francisco Bay Area, where she lives with her partner of twenty-five years, Judy Dlugacz. Rachel is currently working on her memoirs, *Surviving Babylon.* Her published writing includes: "Coming Out of the Frame: Lesbian Feminism and Self Psychology," in *Lesbians in Psychoanalysis* (The Free Press, 1995) and "Hiding is Unhealthy for the Soul," in *Twice Blessed: On Being Lesbian, Gay, and Jewish* (Beacon Press, 1989).

Kyla Wazana Tompkins is a doctoral candidate in the program in modern thought and literature at Stanford University. She is writing her dissertation on food and eating in nineteenth-century literature and in U.S. cultural history, and she has published in *Tikkun,* the *San Francisco Chronicle,* and *Globe and Mail.*

Acknowledgments

Thanks to EJ Khazzoom for borrowing and borrowing (and borrowing) money on my behalf, so I could pursue making this book happen.

Thanks to Rivka Solomon for holding my hand throughout this process and for offering invaluable guidance on how to aggressively and successfully pitch this book.

Thanks to Rachel Wahba for being my personal cheerleader.

Thanks to Michael Larsen for giving me tips on how to write a strong book proposal.

Thanks to Kim Witherspoon for being a role model, placing this book, offering sound advice on all literary matters, and standing 100 percent behind me.

Thanks to David Forrer for countless hours of work on this book, an abundance of support and encouragement, and solid guidance in navigating through procedures.

Thanks to Leslie Miller for recognizing and valuing the vision of this book, being a caring, sensitive, and flexible editor, and offering tremendous enthusiasm.

Thanks to all the professors who took the time to read the manuscript and offer endorsements: Leila Ahmed (Harvard), Rebecca Alpert (Temple), Bettina Aptheker (UC Santa Cruz),

Kwame Anthony Appiah (Harvard), Judith Barker (Ithaca College), Joel Beinin (Stanford), Lila Braine (Barnard), Jill M. Bystydzienski (Iowa State), Janet Chernela (Florida International), Carrie Yang Costello (U. Wisconsin), Joshua Gamson (Princeton), Diana L. Hayes (Georgetown), Janet Jacobs (U. Colorado), Aliza Keddem (Marylhurst), Irena Klepfisz (Barnard), Miriamne Ara Krummel (Lehigh), Becky R. Lee (York), Anne Lapidus Lerner (Jewish Theological Seminary), Yoram Meital (Ben-Gurion), Sonya Michel (U. Illinois), Bonnie J. Morris (George Washington), Margaret O'Neal (East Carolina), Lawrence Rosen (Princeton), Alan Segal (Barnard), Shelly Tenenbaum (Clark), Diane Kholos Wysocki (U. Nebraska).

ABOUT THE EDITOR

Loolwa Khazzoom (www.loolwa.com) pioneered the Jewish multiculturalism movement in 1990, bringing non-European Jewish history, heritage, and social justice concerns into the mainstream Jewish and non-Jewish communities. Her unique emphasis on the psychology of representation, through detailed attention to terminology, has radically transformed dialogue on diversity and Jewish identity, and her work has touched the lives of millions of individuals internationally. Khazzoom's heart-based, accessible approach has catalyzed media interest in Jewish multiculturalism and has inspired the proliferation of countless programs on Jewish diversity. In addition, her focus on community empowerment has helped foster an international network of Jewish multicultural organizations, working together toward a common vision.

Khazzoom founded and directs the Jewish MultiCultural Project, through which she created and implemented the first comprehensive curriculum on Jews around the world. She also has published Jewish multicultural essays in periodicals throughout North America, Israel, Japan, and Germany, including the *New York Times,* the *Washington Post,* the *Los Angeles Times, Rolling Stone, Elle Girl,* and *Marie Claire.* She is also the author of *Consequence: Beyond Resisting Rape* (Pearl In A Million Press, 2001) In addition, Khazzoom is an accomplished musician and has performed traditional North African and Middle Eastern Jewish music at venues internationally.

Selected Titles from Seal Press

Yentl's Revenge: The Next Wave of Jewish Feminism edited by Danya Ruttenberg, foreword by Susannah Heschel. $16.95, 158005-057-3. *Yentl's Revenge* chronicles a range of experiences lived by an entire generation of women, from Judeopagan witches to young Orthodox mothers, from rabbis to sex educators.

Colonize This! Young Women of Color on Today's Feminism edited by Daisy Hernández and Bushra Rehman. $16.95, 1-58005-0670-0. In-your-face, original writing following in the footsteps of *The Bridge Called My Back*.

Listen Up: Voices from the Next Feminist Generation edited by Barbara Findlen. $16.95, 1-58005-054-9. A revised and expanded edition of the Seal Press classic, featuring the voices of a new generation of women expressing the vibrancy and vitality of today's feminist movement.

Body Outlaws: Young Women Write About Body Image and Identity edited by Ophira Edut, foreword by Rebecca Walker. $14.95, 1-58005-043-3. Filled with honesty and humor, this groundbreaking anthology offers stories by women who have chosen to ignore, subvert, or redefine the dominant beauty standard in order to feel at home in their bodies.

Cunt: A Declaration of Independence by Inga Muscio. $14.95, 1-58005-075-1. An ancient title of respect for women, "cunt" long ago veered off the path of honor and now careens toward the heart of every woman as an expletive. Muscio traces this winding road, giving women both the motivation and the tools to claim "cunt" as a positive and powerful force in the lives of all women.

Seal Press publishes many books of fiction and nonfiction by women writers. Please visit our Web site at www.sealpress.com.